MADMEN
AT THE HELM

MADMEN AT THE HELM

Pathology and Politics in the Arab Spring

Muriel Mirak-Weissbach

Garnet PUBLISHING

MADMEN AT THE HELM
Pathology and Politics in the Arab Spring

Published by
Garnet Publishing Limited
8 Southern Court
South Street
Reading
RG1 4QS
UK

www.garnetpublishing.co.uk
www.twitter.com/Garnetpub
www.facebook.com/Garnetpub
blog.garnetpublishing.co.uk

First Paperback Edition

ISBN: 9781859643358

British Library Cataloguing-in-Publication Data
A catalogue record for this book is available from the British Library

Typeset by Samantha Barden
Jacket design by Garnet Publishing

Printed and bound in Lebanon by International Press:
interpress@int-press.com

Contents

Abbreviations

ABC	American Broadcasting Corporation
ASALA	Armenian Secret Army for the Liberation of Armenia
AU	African Union
BBC	British Broadcasting Corporation
CIA	Central Intelligence Agency
COMEST	World Commission on the Ethics of Scientific Knowledge
DNA	Dernières Nouvelles d'Algérie
ETA	Euskadi Ta Askatasuna (Basque separatist organisation)
FAZ	Frankfurter Allgemeine Zeitung
FIS	Front Islamique du Salut (Islamic Salvation Front)
FSA	Free Syrian Army
GCC	Gulf Cooperation Council
GPC	General People's Congress
IAEA	International Atomic Energy Agency
ICC	International Criminal Court
IMF	International Monetary Fund
IRA	Irish Republican Army
JMP	Joint Meeting Parties
NATO	North Atlantic Treaty Organisation
NDP	National Democratic Party
NTC	National Transitional Council
PFLP	Popular Front for the Liberation of Palestine
PFLP-GC	Popular Front for the Liberation of Palestine – General Command
PNF	Progressive National Front
RCD	Rassemblement Constitutionnel Démocratique
SABA	Yemen news agency
SIS	State Information Service
SISMI	Servizio per le Informazioni e la Sicurezza Militare (Italian military intelligence service)
SNC	Syrian National Council
UGTT	Union Générale Tunisienne du Travail (Tunisian General Labour Union)

Acknowledgements

I would like to thank Professor Mohammad Seyyed Selim and Professor Elaine Hagopian for providing insightful background material as well as referring me to further sources. Dr Jack Danielian, PhD, psychologist and psychiatrist, gave me help in defining certain technical terminology and suggesting further sources in the study of personality disorders. My brother Bob again proved to be a careful and creative reader in reviewing the early drafts of this book. My thanks also to my husband, Michael, for being so supportive and maintaining an atmosphere of calm. All their contributions were vital; however, the assessments and conclusions in this study are solely those of the author.

Frontispiece

Ghadaffi: 'If we are faced with a madman like [the Jordanian King] Hussein who wants to kill his people we must send someone to seize him, handcuff him, stop him from doing what he's doing and take him off to an asylum.'

King Feisal: 'I don't think you should call an Arab king a madman who should be taken to an asylum.'

Ghadaffi: 'But all his family are mad. It's a matter of record.'

King Feisal: 'Well, perhaps all of us are mad.'

Nasser: 'Sometimes when you see what is going on in the Arab world, your Majesty, I think this may be so. I suggest we appoint a doctor to examine us regularly and find out which ones are crazy.'

King Feisal: 'I would like your doctor to start with me, because in view of what I see I doubt whether I shall be able to preserve my reason.'

Cairo Conference, September 1970[1]

NOTES

—

1 Heikal, Mohamed, *The Road to Ramadan*, William Collins Sons & Co. Ltd., London, 1975, p. 100.

Introduction

When, in late December 2010, thousands of Tunisians took to the streets demanding that President Zine El-Abidine Ben Ali step down and pave the way for the introduction of a representative government, most of the world gasped in disbelief and persons in high places in governments feared the worst. Yet, the '2011 Revolution' succeeded – even at the cost of too many civilian lives cut short by regime bullets – and an authoritarian regime that had ruled for decades had to bow out and make room for a transitional government which would oversee elections leading to the first democratically elected parliament and government in well over a half a century.

Citizens in Egypt, energized by the Tunisian precedent, launched their own revolt and, after weeks of political mobilization, succeeded in bringing down the regime of 'the last Pharaoh', Hosni Mubarak. Yemen and Libya soon joined the Arab revolution and protests broke out even in the entrenched monarchies, emirates and sheikdoms of Jordan and the Persian Gulf. Syria was next to be rocked by social convulsions.

The economic–social motivations for such dramatic upheaval across the Arab world have been identified widely: high unemployment (especially among the youth, who make up the majority of the population); a widening gap between the very rich (those who have benefited from the despotic regimes' rampant corruption and mafia-style economies) and the very poor (some, in Egypt, living on less than US$2 a day); dictatorial rule over decades, with emergency laws allowing for arbitrary arrests and lengthy detention without charges brought; torture of political prisoners, estimated to range in the tens of thousands, and so forth.

This wretched state of affairs had prevailed for decades without effective opposition. Then suddenly – or so it seemed to observers and foreign intelligence services who had not done their homework – people took to the streets. In reality, it was not at all so sudden. Opposition movements in Tunisia, Egypt and elsewhere, though savagely repressed, had not ceased to exist and, manoeuvring within the confines of police states, had managed to maintain contact with like-minded individuals and groups organized in loose networks. In Tunisia, civil society organizations had emerged and flourished, benefiting from Ben Ali's PR campaign aimed at convincing the West that he was liberalizing his land politically. Although these associations wielded no political power, they did provide the means for citizens to come together in a social web, which would then represent the organizing energy for the revolution.

In Egypt, for over ten years opposition groups had moved into whatever space was afforded them. True, the revolution that erupted in January 2011 was triggered by events in Tunisia, but the opposition had actually been organizing itself in Egypt since 2000. The second Palestinian Intifada and the Iraq war provoked demonstrations at Cairo University between 2000 and 2004; in the following year, when parliamentary elections took place, widespread fraud occurred. The Kifaya movement came into being, after former Malaysian Prime Minister Mahathir Mohamed, on a visit to Cairo, told a press conference that he had resigned as prime minister because '22 years are enough'. 'Enough' – Kifaya – became the name of a robust opposition movement to Mubarak. In 2006–2007 strikes broke out against IMF-dictated privatization; in 2006 demonstrators expressed solidarity with Lebanon and, in 2008, with Gazans against Israeli aggressions. In 2008, the April 6 youth movement came into being as a strike-support committee for workers opposing privatization programmes. Then, in 2010, when the issue of presidential elections appeared on the agenda, an 'ElBaradei for President' movement emerged, along with the 'We are all Khaled Said' movement, led by Wael Ghonim; Khaled Said is the name of an Egyptian blogger who was brutally tortured and killed by Egyptian security services in June 2010. At the same time, so-called parliamentary elections took place and were so thoroughly rigged that even the few token opposition Members of Parliament allowed to sit there found their ranks decimated. The social-economic-political climate was simmering, and all that was needed was a match to ignite the protest.[1] That match was lit in Tunisia.

What triggered the uprising in Tunisia was highly symbolic. A man, though equipped with a baccalaureate, had found no other means to support his widowed mother and seven siblings than to hawk vegetables on a cart. When a policewoman controlled Mohammad Bouazizi's papers one day and found he had no 'licence', she slapped him in the face, insulted his dead father and shut down his trade. Although accounts of the encounter with the policewoman have been disputed, it is confirmed that he appealed to the governor's office for redress, and was rudely rebuffed. He doused himself with petrol, set himself on fire and died of his burns 18 days later. What might be misconstrued as the gesture of a desperate individual was in reality a tragic event epitomizing the plight of an entire population. It was the act of a man who decided to sacrifice himself to send a message to the powers that be that, to preserve his dignity as a human being, he would rather die than submit to such arbitrary humiliation. Although President Ben Ali visited the man in the hospital, no such paternalistic gesture could stem the outrage of the population.[2]

Bouazizi's sacrifice will go down in history alongside the sacrifice of Czech student Jan Palach, whose self-immolation in 1969 inspired anti-communist protest, or, reaching back farther in time, certain landmarks of the American civil rights movement of the 1960s: it was the decision of one Rosa Parks to defend her dignity as a human being rather than give up her seat on a bus to a white that suddenly catalysed mass action eventually leading to the abolition of the apartheid regime against black Americans. A psychological analysis of the Bouazizi incident has characterized it as a narcissistic affront to his dignity, which was felt by the population as an affront to all, not only the individual.[3]

What fuelled the Egyptian revolution was this moral/political issue raised by Bouazizi. Mohammad Seyyed Selim, an Egyptian professor friend and well-known intellectual, told me in the first days of the demonstrations that what mobilized Egyptian youth was not the economic misery *per se* that their generation had suffered but the social and psychological degradation that accompanied it. Egyptian youth, he told me, 'can endure deprivation, but not humiliation'. He had forecast in an article in *Al Arabi* on 23 January that Egypt would follow the Tunisian course because the two countries shared the same conditions. A similar phenomenon has been manifest in the various uprisings (Intifadas) by Palestinians in the West Bank and Gaza: they were rejecting not only the Israeli occupation of their lands, but also the theft of their dignity as human beings.

This is the decisive subjective factor in the movement's success: young Egyptians who launched the demonstrations showed the courage to defy the regime and its police state apparatus. After the Tunisian events, they overcame the fear that had held them and their compatriots in captive passivity over decades. When the regime responded with police attacks, and the first reports of casualties surfaced, the movement maintained the moral high ground. It did not respond with violence, but continued to expand the mobilization. Dr Gerhard Fulda, a former German diplomat who happened to be in Cairo when the revolution erupted, recalled being in Tahrir Square on the day the security police opened fire on the crowd. Although, as he told a gathering of the German–Arab Society in Berlin on 26 February, he no longer considered himself a religious man and had not visited his local church for years, he did utter a silent prayer at that moment. The gist of it was: please God let them not respond with violence. Thank God, he reported, the masses of protesters did *not* respond with violence, and that decided the outcome of the revolution. It was, in fact, the principled commitment to non-violent civil disobedience that determined the outcome in Tunisia and Egypt.[4]

The Social Psychology of the Revolutionary Process

Anyone who followed the developments over those days and weeks experienced something new on the horizon, first in Tunisia, then in Egypt. Young people were standing up for their rights and articulating their demands in unprecedented form. 'Ben Ali must go' shouted the protesters in Tunis; 'Mubarak must go' was the cry in Cairo; then, the regime must go, the emergency laws must be repealed, a new constitution and new elections must follow. In Yemen, it was: 'Saleh, leave!' and in Libya, 'Down with Qaddafi!' Syrians initially demonstrated for democratic reforms, then, after meeting with police brutality, escalated their slogans to call for regime change.

So much for the formal political demands. The power in the stance of the demonstrators derived from their willingness to put their lives on the line for the cause. What they told worldwide TV audiences via satellite stations, whether militantly or quite calmly, was: I will stay here and demonstrate until we prevail. I will stay here until I die if necessary. One young man looking straight into the camera said: 'It's a question of freedom or death.' He may never have heard of the orator and politician Patrick Henry's famous utterance 'Give me liberty or give me death', but he transmitted the same message. Martin Luther King believed that for a person to know what it means to be human, he must be ready to die for a cause. As he put it, 'If a man hasn't discovered something he will die for, he isn't fit to live.' In the course of the Arab revolt, the youth were discovering what it means to be human.

This constitutes a fundamental revolution in thinking. History has shown in the American civil rights movement of the 1960s, or more recently in the peaceful revolution of the East German population in 1989, that when a people declares it is ready to die for its cause, there is no weapon capable of defeating it – short of mass murder. When American civil rights leader Amelia Boynton Robinson led a march on the Alabama state capital on 7 March 1965, so that Black Americans might gain the right to vote, she and her colleagues put their lives on the line. Police on horseback, flanked by vicious dogs, attacked them ferociously in what was to become famous as Bloody Sunday. They won the right to vote.

The key to victory was the opposition's commitment to non-violent resistance, no matter how high the death toll. In Egypt, it was more than 800, and yet they did not desist. Figures on casualties in Libya and Syria have yet to be defined. As one young Arab put it, 'They can't kill us all.' When, conversely, the opposition abandoned civil disobedience and (for whatever reasons) opted for armed resistance as in Libya and Syria, it not only lost the moral high ground but became increasingly prey to geopolitical manipulation.

The 'new Arabs' have been born in this historic process. They are people from all walks of life, all social strata, all religious faiths. What unites them is a revolutionary fervour to usher in a new system of government, committed to democracy and equal rights for all citizens before the law. The TV interviews with the youth document that they have assumed a new political, moral and historical identity. One told CNN and other satellite stations' cameramen: 'I have lived for decades in fear and trepidation; now that is gone and I finally know that I am a human being, with dignity and rights.' One of the loudest slogans to be heard on 11 February, when Mubarak had left, was: '*Irfa rasak, anta misri!* [Hold your head high, you are an Egyptian!]'

This is the real change that has occurred. Not the ouster of a hated dictator *per se* – although that was the precondition – but the shift in outlook on the part of an entire population, especially the youth, who had been depressed and passive. Anyone who has visited Cairo over the past ten years as I have can recall the images of demoralization and despair. In front of every shop or public building in Cairo sat an old man in a battered kaftan, sipping tea and earning his couple of Egyptian pounds per day by 'guarding' the building. Serving him tea was a young Egyptian boy who should have been in school, but instead was earning a pittance by working as a pavement waiter. In front of banks, hotels and other large buildings were soldiers, police and their official vehicles. Whether it was the national television building or the headquarters of the Arab League or any ministry, everywhere the police and military maintained a very visible and, at times, intimidating presence. Hotel personnel were often obsequious, fawning over guests in hopes of a decent tip. Street vendors, like bazaaris, descended upon foreign visitors like vultures, intent on extracting whatever bounty there might be, while scrawny cats fought over tidbits fallen from a tourist's table.

Much the same dreary scenery greeted the visitor to Tunisia. When I was there in 1994, I was shocked by the number of police and other security personnel on every block; there seemed to be more of them than there are cafés in any Italian city. And the overkill in numbers of agents deployed was responsible for a surrealistic level of intimidation of the population. A friend whom I visited then, who was a journalist and human rights activist, was so used to being overheard or taped by the omnipresent security units that she rolled down the convertible top of her car and lowered all windows before telling me in confidence how oppressive the police state regime was. Her name was Sihem Bensedrine, later to become an inspiration for the revolution.

Through their mass uprising against such oppressive rule, citizens in key Arab nations succeeded in ridding themselves of these archaic dictatorships. Not only was the Egyptian revolution a political event, but also it was a moral watershed. The same must be said of the Tunisian developments and the upsurges in Yemen, Libya and Syria. Even in Benghazi, the stronghold of the Libyan opposition, a remarkable social transformation unfolded, as citizens united in an effort to support their troops on the front. Volunteers in Benghazi breached earlier social taboos whereby women and men should work in parallel but not together, as members of both sexes rolled up their sleeves and worked side by side. Women took a leading role in organizing food rations, which would be taken by men to the fighters on the front; young men presented themselves to the volunteer women offering the assistance of their female relatives. Although Qaddafi had preached his bizarre concept of relations between the sexes in society, this was the first time that

Libyan men and women had experienced equality. In Yemen, a very traditional society, women also emerged as protagonists of the movement and one of them, Tawakul Karman, received the Nobel Peace Prize for her efforts.

Youth Challenges an Ageing Decadent Order

This was the healthy side of the process.

While freedom lovers worldwide were applauding the Arab revolution, the regimes under fire were fighting for their very lives. First Ben Ali, then Mubarak, then Saleh, Qaddafi and Assad stubbornly clung to power and would not face the fact that the entire world had written them off. They categorically snubbed appeals to resign for the good of their people and nation.

The would-be 'presidents for life' challenged by popular uprisings share more than one common denominator.[5] They (or their dynasties) had been in power for decades (four of them for over 30 years), and had erected repressive dictatorial regimes based on special forces, interior ministry police and intelligence agencies. They had governed through recourse to emergency rule, which allowed them to smother any whisper of opposition, hauled off opposition figures to jails where torture chambers awaited them and periodically orchestrated the charade of 'elections', in which the vote for the ruling elite wavered between 95 per cent and 98 per cent – results that former East German dictator Erich Honecker would have envied. Enjoying a monopoly on power, they had exploited their political status to amass vast personal fortunes through corruption, diversion of foreign aid, shares in state-controlled economic enterprise and so forth. The enormous levels of wealth brought into their private possession had been deposited variously in foreign bank accounts (later, happily, frozen by host countries).

Despite decades of oppressive police state rule their people did not lose their human dignity and, when the opportunity presented itself, they moved. It was a generational shift. The youth up to 25–30 years old, who had known literally nothing in their lifetimes but the *status quo* – i.e. the eternal presidents – did however know that what they experienced in daily life was not a universal phenomenon. Many of them had visited Europe or studied there, or had friends who had travelled abroad and, even if not, had access through the Internet to news about the outside world. It was this generation of young people who led the surge against the senile, antiquated regime. It was a revolt by healthy, future-oriented youth against a dying dictatorial order.

The contrast could not be more dramatic: on the one hand, thousands, then tens of thousands, then, yes, millions of citizens of all walks of life were streaming into the centre of Tunis or Cairo and Sana'a, peacefully demanding their rights not only as citizens of a specific nation but as human beings endowed with inalienable rights, citizens embracing members of the armed forces who had made the right moral choice and joined the demonstrators. AlJazeera and others broadcast images of young men brimming with pride holding up their infant children, whom they had brought to the central squares to allow them to take part in what they knew were historic events. Young girls in headscarves were filmed riding on the back of mopeds, their faces beaming with hope and their hands raised in the victory sign.

Opposite them were the stony-faced old men in power – Ben Ali, Mubarak or Saleh, or the wild-eyed Colonel Qaddafi, as well as the anomalous younger Assad, the second generation representative of an autocratic dynasty – in clinical denial of the reality their people had confronted them with, attempting, first, to appease the masses with pathetic promises of 'reform', then, threatening dire consequences if the protests continued, even to the point of civil war, and finally vowing to uphold their bankrupt positions of power to the bitter end. Their attitude was: *après moi, le déluge* and, in the extreme case of Qaddafi, the message was that, if he were to be removed from power, he would inflict the maximum damage on his people, taking as many with him to the grave as possible. Qaddafi proved true to his word, and unleashed inordinate force against his own people in a conflict that developed into a bloody civil war with tens of thousands of victims.

The bitter end came for some sooner, for others later.

In the uprisings, two diametrically opposed but mutually reinforcing social–psychological dynamics unfolded: the more the leader exerted authoritarian rule by ordering security forces to open fire on the crowd, the more the protesters mobilized, expanding their numbers by the day. The more the rebels would organize their resistance, the more intransigent the ruler would become threatening greater repression, and the more the opposition would expand its support base … and so on and so forth. And in response, the political leadership would escalate its violence, stubbornly asserting its legitimacy and power. In the process, it would lose all legitimacy and ultimately all power.

What was crucial in the cases of Tunisia and Egypt was the stance of the military. Displaying an uncanny political maturity, demonstrators appealed to the military to join them to protect them from armed assaults by the regime's special police forces. As members of draft armies, these soldiers could not and would not obey orders to kill their own brethren. Qaddafi, apparently aware of this principle, had long since given special forces a privileged position with his regular army and later recruited mercenaries to shore up his dictatorship. In Syria, the Assad dynasty had forged a symbiosis of the army, the Ba'ath Party and the security apparatus which did not hesitate to open fire on protesters in the streets. But the time came when soldiers and officers defected and formed the Free Syrian Army (FSA). In Tunisia and Egypt, it was also sheer numbers that tipped the balance. No matter how many people the regime could assemble, no matter how many killers it could deploy, it came to the point that the protesters literally outnumbered the government forces.

Geopoliticians Take Over

Intersecting these two sociological processes was a third dynamic, geopolitical in nature. It was as if opposing forces were playing out their separate but intertwining narratives on a stage, when an intruder thrust himself into the director's chair, ripped the screenplay to shreds and proceeded to dictate moves according to his own script. The walk-ons suddenly mushroomed in number and assumed roles of protagonists.

Although in the course of 2012 it became common in some circles to dismiss the entire Arab revolution as a geopolitical conspiracy, the matter is more complex. Bouazizi was not following orders from a Western intelligence agency, nor were Egyptian youth. But, as the originally organic protest movements approached their aims, other foreign-based forces intervened to lend decisive advantage to their assets and hijack the process. Thus in Egypt, the US-backed military assumed special powers and, in a negotiated arrangement, divided power with the Muslim Brotherhood. Thus, the US worked through the Gulf Cooperation Council to stage-manage the Yemeni president's departure from the scene.

The most blatant and bloody instances of geopolitical manipulation occurred in Libya and Syria. The United Nations Security Council resolution which paved the way for NATO's war of aggression against Libya was not only of dubious legality but constituted a challenge to Russia and China, whose governments were to wield their power of veto in subsequent cases. In Syria, the civil war assumed the character of a full-fledged geostrategic conflict, a proxy war between the West and its regional allies Saudi Arabia, Qatar and Turkey, on the one hand, and Russia and China, flanked by Syria's regional allies Hezbollah, Iran and Shi'ite formations in Iraq and elsewhere, on the other.

Those geopolitical agencies attempting to steer events had detailed plans for reorganizing the entire Middle East region on their drawing boards for decades and pulled them out for implementation once the protests had erupted. Several of the scenarios drafted for regime change in the region date back to the end of the Cold War, when neoconservatives in the US authored new strategic doctrine papers aimed at establishing the US as the sole remaining superpower. Among these documents was a 1996 blueprint for consolidating nuclear power Israel as the regional hegemonic force, and changing regimes deemed to threaten this design, from Iraq to Syria, Lebanon to Iran. The 2003 war against Iraq, the 2005–2006 destabilizations of Lebanon and Syria, Israel's war on Gaza in 2008, etc. dovetailed with this project.[6]

At the same time in 2007, the Bush administration 'redirected' its regional policy, cooperating with the Saudis and Sunni extremist groups in an effort to undermine Iran. These groups included not only members of the Muslim Brotherhood and Salafists, but armed militants associated with Al Qaida. The hostile posture towards the Islamic Republic included operations to weaken Syria and Hezbollah.[7] This new thrust by the Bush administration was bequeathed to his successor and when the upsurges began in North Africa, sectors of the US foreign policy establishment remained allied to the most extremist Sunni elements, including those who would take up arms in Syria. Thus, although the protests were not triggered by Washington, it was locked into an embrace with the political and, later, military protagonists of the insurrection.

Such is the complex nature of the geopolitical dimension of the events in the Arab uprisings. But it is not the primary focus of this book, which instead highlights the psychological element.

Politics and Pathology

To comprehend the behaviour of the Arab political leaders challenged by demands for social and political change, I suggest undertaking a clinical examination of the psychological personality disorders present. Mubarak and Qaddafi *et al.* are not only discrete personalities; they also represent 'types' which the relevant professional psychoanalytical literature can illuminate.[8] In the case of the leaders of these Arab nations overtaken by revolution, we are probably dealing with several different types of personality disorder: from the narcissistic to the paranoid.

Since the ground-breaking work of Sigmund Freud, there has been a plethora of important studies published that examine various aspects of this complex matter. Psychoanalysts documented their clinical experience with cases of narcissism, paranoia, hysteria and psychopathy – all relevant phenomena to the political personalities examined here – and some researchers have directly investigated the appearance of such psychological disturbances in the realm of political life. This area of research, known as 'psycho-historical studies' and 'applied psychoanalysis', seeks to employ an understanding of pathological personality structures to specific cases of political leadership figures.[9]

Here, I intend to utilize the results of such studies – especially the analytical approach that they adopt – to examine the behaviour of the various heads of state in the Arab world during the revolutionary process. This study is based on the chronicle of events, and focuses on the actions, speeches and public statements of the protagonists as the dramatic events unfolded. Background material on the individual political figures, particularly regarding their family histories, childhood experiences and adult education and training, is of utmost relevance in comprehending the genesis of pathology in power.

But we are not dealing only with discrete personalities, their personal histories and careers. They are all embedded in a cultural matrix, which has seen the influence of outside forces shaping reality. The Arabs have not had an easy time of it, to put it mildly. The much sought-after Arab unity has been a chimera, largely due to the determination of the Great Powers – Great Britain, the US and France – to crush it.

After four centuries under Ottoman rule, the Arabs sought independence at the time of the First World War, but were manipulated by the European powers that pretended to back their rebellion. France and Britain signed a secret agreement, the Sykes-Picot accord, to divide up the oil-rich territory between them and, though the secret was exposed by the Soviets, the post-First World War order reflected this scheme. Most of the leaders of the newly carved Arab nations on the map were hand-picked by those European powers and functioned largely as heads of puppet states. Even when nationalist movements arose to throw off the colonial yoke, led by men who became national heroes, the new leaders rapidly introduced mechanisms for top-down control over their people and nations.

More to the point, their leaders more often than not were backed by Western powers. The Italians played a key role in Qaddafi's 1969 coup as well as in Ben Ali's seizure of power in 1987. Although Nasser does not fit into this category, his successor Anwar Sadat became a crucial ally of the United States through the Camp David peace with Israel, and since that time Egypt has depended on American money and backing. Yemen has enjoyed foreign backing in its fight against terrorism and the Assad dynasty had received for a certain time the support of the West as a bulwark of stability in the historically unstable Middle East.

Although the stimulus for the current study was provided by the 2010–2011 Arab rebellions, the analyses and conclusions are not limited to their experience. Presented in the form of a postscript is a brief reference to two cases of narcissism in contemporary American politics. On the one hand, there's George W. Bush, whose eight-year reign betrays the indelible marks of a severe personality disorder. As the clinical study by Dr Justin Frank[10] documented in detail, the US president was an emotionally disturbed individual and should never have been allowed to hold that high office in the United States. Dr Frank, a psychiatrist and Professor of Psychology at George Washington University, based his work on a professional analysis of the public statements by Bush, viewed in light of his traumatized childhood experience.

Similar psychological syndromes appear in the cases of certain American political sects and personality cults masquerading as political organizations, as well as in the relatively new phenomenon of the Tea Party movement, whose leader, Sarah Palin, offers another clinical case study.

NOTES

—

1   Mirak-Weissbach, Muriel, 'The Birth of the New Egyptians', *Global Research*, 15 February 2011, http://www.globalresearch.ca/index.php?context=va&aid=23231; Amin, Galal, *Egypt in the Era of Hosni Mubarak 1981–2011*, The American University in Cairo Press, Cairo, New York, 2011; Al Aswany, Alaa, *On the State of Egypt: What Made the Revolution Inevitable*, translation by Jonathan Wright, Vintage Books, Random House, New York, April 2011.

2   Bouazizi was not the first Tunisian to commit suicide as a sign of social protest, but his death precipitated events due to the popular response to it. Members of the teachers' trade union were the ones who took the burning man to the hospital and who alerted his family. It was the UGTT unions that termed the suicide a 'political assassination' and formed committees that put the protest process into motion. Angrist, Michele Penner, 'Old Grievances and New Opportunities; Understanding the Tunisian Revolution', Middles East Studies Association (MESA) conference, Washington, DC, 3 December 2011.

3   Benslama, Fethi, *Soudain la révolution! De la Tunisie au monde arabe: la signification d'un soulèvement*, Éditions Denoël, Paris, 2011, cited by Silvia Marsans-Sakly, 'The Making and Meaning of an Event', MESA conference, ibid.

4   'Special Report: Inside the Egyptian Revolution', 13 April 2011, Nonviolent Action Network; Sharp, Gene, *From Dictatorship to Democracy: A Conceptual Framework for Liberation*, The Albert Einstein Institution, Fourth US Edition, Boston, 2010.

5   Owen, Roger, *The Rise and Fall of Arab Presidents for Life*, Harvard University Press, Cambridge, May 2012.

6   'A Clean Break: A New Strategy for Securing the Realm', www.iasps.org/strat1.htm. The authors were Dick Cheney's aide David Wurmser and his wife Meyrav, Richard Perle, James Colbert, Charles Fairbanks Jr., Douglas Feith, Robert Loewenberg, Jonathan Torop, among others.

7   Hersh, Seymour M. 'The Redirection: Is the Administration's new policy befitting our enemies in the war on terrorism?' *The New Yorker*, 5 March 2007.

8   See bibliography for references to professional psychoanalytical literature consulted.

9   Historical figures who have been examined from this standpoint include numerous Roman emperors, especially Caligula and Nero, as well as Napoleon, Mussolini, Stalin and so on.

10   Frank, Justin A., M.D., *Bush on the Couch: Inside the Mind of the President*, ReganBooks, an imprint of HarperCollins Publishers, New York, NY, 2004, 2005.

1

Narcissus on the Throne

To appreciate the conduct of the leaders of the five nations under consideration here – Tunisia, Egypt, Yemen, Libya and Syria – we need to examine them from a clinical standpoint. Political analysts from think-tanks, senior foreign correspondents and intelligence specialists worldwide will put their own particular twist on the reasons why Egyptian President Hosni Mubarak waited so long after mass demonstrations had engulfed his country before he dared speak to the nation, or why Tunisian President Zine El-Abidine Ben Ali chose to address his citizenry in the local dialect instead of classical high Arabic. Mubarak, they will say, was playing a waiting game, buying time, so to speak; and Ben Ali was merely adopting the idiom of the people, to bridge the gap between the presidency and the populace. In neither case did it work. But that is not the point.

Such explanations are, at best, naive. To grasp the reasons for the extraordinary and at times outrageous comportment of these leaders under siege, we have to leave the familiar, comfortable world of journalistic clichés and delve into the realm of clinical psychology – to be more precise, applied psychoanalysis. No matter what immediate political considerations might appear to motivate the leader's move at any point along the way, it is deep-rooted psychological factors that can more fully explain the words and actions of these individuals.

In most of the cases under consideration here, we are dealing with what clinical psychoanalytical literature calls the *narcissistic personality*. As first analysed by Sigmund Freud, not only is narcissism a pathological manifestation that can appear in diverse personality types, but also it is most frequently encountered among political figures, especially those elevated to a position of power.[1] Narcissism and power, as we shall discover, are closely related; on the one hand, the narcissistic personality strives to attain power in order to satisfy a pathological need for admiration, recognition and love, and, on the other hand, even the 'normal' person who comes to occupy a position of power may tend, as a result, to develop narcissistic traits as a quasi-'natural' expression of his political function.

Where does the term come from? Ancient Greek lore relates the myth of one Narcissus, a 16-year-old whose extraordinary beauty overwhelmed other youth and even himself. Echo, a nymph, was one of the many who fell in love with the handsome young man. As her name indicates, she echoed the words of others, but could not speak herself. She tried once to offer her love to Narcissus, but out of pride he rejected her, and she ultimately turned into stone. One day while he was out hunting, Narcissus looked for water to quench his thirst, and came upon a spring. When he knelt down and looked into the water, he saw his reflection and fell in love with it. Vainly he kissed the water, only to realize this was a mirror image of himself. After pining away for this impossible love, Narcissus died, and a flower by that name grew where he perished.[2]

Whatever the details of the many variations on the myth, the essence of narcissism is self-love, which entails a number of attributes. Narcissists typically have an overly exaggerated estimation of themselves and their capabilities – their 'grandiose self'.[3] They require the admiration of others – those who reassure them of their grandiosity.

Otto F. Kernberg described the narcissistic personality as 'characterized by an abnormally extreme self-idealization to the extent of incorporating ideal components of others'. This 'self-idealization' allows the individual to assert a sense of self-sufficiency and independence. His 'exaggerated amount of grandiosity and self-centeredness' may give way to inferiority feelings if this image is challenged. In general, '[t]he pathological grandiose self of the patients – an expression of an abnormal self-idealization – shows up in exhibitionism, an entitlement mentality, ruthlessness, ... a chronic tendency to devalue others, exploitative and parasitical behaviour ...' The narcissist has to be the centre of attention, where he (or she) enjoys admiration from all onlookers.[4]

In the case of political leaders, they have to surround themselves with 'yes-men', adulators and flatterers, who assure them to no end that they are always right. They need to feel loved and feared, and will not tolerate any criticism. Persons exhibiting any independent judgement are to be shunned. Anyone who dares to criticize the narcissistic leader or question his authority will be subjected to massive social pressure. In the psychological group dynamic, an 'in-group' of avid supporters will rally to the leader, and protect him from any of the critics, who are known as the 'out-group'.[5]

Such psychological insight explains why narcissistic leaders insist on total control over public opinion especially through the means of mass communication. Not only is press censorship widespread, but journalists may risk their lives if they criticize the leader or his policies. A prerequisite for a dictatorial regime under this psychological type is a robust and ruthless police force, combined with an internal security apparatus capable of monitoring citizens' behaviour, and spacious prison facilities fitted out with torture chambers.

The people should not only fear the ruler, but worship him as well. To this end, he erects and nurtures a personality cult. Public images of the leader are crucial to imposing the sense of his presumed superiority. How many capital cities in dictatorial regimes have their avenues lined with larger-than-life portraits of the leader or pharaonic statues in tasteless neo-Stalinist style? Other trappings include palatial estates used as presidential residences, immense villas for holiday retreats, kilometre-long motorcades throughout the capital whenever the leader passes through, frequent public events celebrating the leader and his accomplishments, events to which thousands of cheering supporters are organized. Very visible, massive security is deployed on all such occasions to advertise the perceived threat level.

The narcissistic leader expects special treatment at all times, and makes sure that he receives it. On his foreign visits, Colonel Qaddafi, for example, always demanded that his hosts accommodate him and his extensive entourage in a large tent in the vicinity of the deluxe hotel where other heads of state resided in normal executive suites.

The narcissist not only exaggerates his own capabilities, but also tends to think of himself as a god. Referring to the Roman emperor Caligula, psychoanalyst Hans-Jürgen Wirth analyses this 'illusion of being godlike, a ruler over life and death. However,' he points out, 'the problem of the ruler who has all the power on earth is that he cannot avoid realizing the limits of his power, that is, the limits, frailty and vulnerability of his own life.' Everyone is, after all, mortal. Wirth goes on: 'The more the megalomaniac ruler gives in to his illusion of being like God, the more he isolates himself from his fellows and from reality. This again leads to paranoid fears and persecution mania, which he answers with another increase in his narcissistic fantasies of grandeur.' When thus detached from reality, he may seek protection in 'chronic hostility, coldness, presumption, sarcasm and a general contempt for mankind'.[6] He has nothing but disdain for others, and speaks of them in abusive, insulting terms. This hostility can extend to what Heinz Kohut calls 'chronic narcissistic rage', which generates acts of vendetta.[7] It is in a state of such rage that narcissistic dictators may commit atrocities on a mass scale – like ordering security units to fire live ammunition at peaceful protesters.

Even outside the public arena, in interpersonal relations, the narcissist will always seek to occupy centre stage to exalt his grandiosity in hopes of gaining the admiration of others.[8] He is extremely jealous of others, always fearing someone else might steal the limelight. In social contact with other human beings, he is exploitative, treating people as mere tools of his power and, when they have served their purpose, discarding them like used tissues. He displays no capacity whatever for empathy, whether in the case of another individual or entire populations.

His paranoia can be extreme, and he views anyone else as a potential enemy and threat. Kernberg calls the syndrome of a leader who combines such narcissism and paranoia 'malignant narcissism', which is very often found in dictators. 'This syndrome,' he writes, 'is defined by the combination of (1) a narcissistic personality disorder, (2) antisocial behaviour, (3) ego-syntonic aggression or sadism directed against others … and (4) a strong paranoid orientation.' It is due to his paranoia that he needs to surround himself with 'yes-men', subjects who will express love and admiration in a spirit of unquestioned loyalty.[9] Thinking always in black-and-white terms, he divides the world into (potential) enemies and loyal friends; in the same categorical manner, he draws a rigid line between Good and Evil. If he perceives the enemy as particularly dangerous, threatening his very survival, he will justify unleashing total force against him, and will derive sadistic pleasure from the most gruesome, barbarous acts.

Among the various styles of leadership encountered in narcissistic personalities, there are those who require followers to be totally obedient to their orders.[10] This type will insist on micromanaging everything, refusing to delegate authority because of mistrust and may fly into a rage if any decisions at any level are made without his explicit approval.

Because of his constant need for gratification through flattery, admiration and general social/political support, the narcissistic ruler is utterly incapable of contemplating the possibility that 'his people' may turn against him. His obsession with himself blinds him to social processes in the real world, and he continues to nurture the illusion that his people love him. This was the case with the Romanian dictator Ceausescu and the East German Communist leader Erich Honecker.[11] Or, recall Qaddafi's adamant insistence in an interview on 28 February 2011 with Christiane Amanpour on ABC: 'All my people love me. They would die to protect me.'

Hysteria and Sociopathy

This trait bears similarities to the *hysterical personality* (more recently referred to as the *histrionic personality*), a psychological disorder examined in depth by psychoanalyst Fritz Riemann.[12] Several of the deposed Arab heads of state conform to this personality structure which fears and rejects anything that smacks of finality, inevitability, necessity – anything, in short, which may limit the individual's illusion of being all-powerful. He who suffers from clinical hysteria will struggle to stave off natural processes, like that of becoming old. To defeat the ageing process, or at least its visible signs, he may resort to plastic surgery or hair dyes, as in the cases of Qaddafi, and Mubarak and Ben Ali, respectively.

Faced with those final, inevitable realities of our lives, which are indeed old age and death, the hysterical personality will 'attempt to sustain as long as possible the illusion of eternal youth and the idea of a future still before them full of all kinds of opportunities'.[13] In the case of the Arab politicians under consideration, this sheds light on their insistence on remaining president for life, and rewriting constitutions to make that possible. It is as if they clung to a quasi-superstitious belief that, as long as they remained in power, even Death could not remove them.

Hysterical personalities, when under attack, will try to turn the tables on their attackers, often resorting to conspiracy theories. Thus, as demonstrators took to the streets *en masse* against the Egyptian *rais*, he and the state media issued the line that it was outside agitators, foreigners and terrorists who were sowing discord. Qaddafi followed suit with the claim that Al Qaida had distributed psychedelic drugs to Libyan youth and unleashed them against their benevolent master. Ali Abdullah Saleh asserted that there was a command centre in Tel Aviv which was orchestrating demonstrations in Sana'a, and that the Israeli command was receiving instructions from Washington. Bashar al-Assad's consistent reactions to public demonstrations echoed this line. Riemann writes that when an individual realizes his shortcomings and guilt, then 'an "enemy" is particularly suited to such projections, and one has the impression that enemies must be invented for discharging one's own guilt'[14] – guilt, in this case, for having ordered violence against one's own people.

This feature resembles the narcissist's need to define an enemy image, which he can identify as the source of all threats. And, like the narcissist, the hysterical personality will seek a form of defence in self-glorification, coming across as the 'first fiddle'. This tendency increases as the insecurity between one's real identity and one's presumed identity becomes evident.[15] Such was manifest in public statements by the besieged rulers who played up their past exploits and service as 'father of the nation' or decorated military heroes. 'In their case, the office or dignity is less of a duty than is the case with the compulsive persons; rather it is the opportunity to heighten the glamour of their personality which is why medals and titles are particularly attractive to them'.[16]

Yet another phenomenon to be considered is that of the *antisocial personality disorder*. Persons suffering this disorder, in more extreme forms referred to as *sociopaths* or *psychopaths*, incorporate narcissism but display several additional traits, the most salient being the lack of truthfulness or pathological lying. What makes this personality structure difficult to diagnose is the superficial appearance of total normality in the person, according to Dr Hervey Cleckley, who has investigated this disorder in depth. The sociopath is of average or, more often than not, superior intelligence, and can be extremely charming and affable. 'Alert and friendly in his attitude, he is easy to talk with and seems to have a good many genuine interests. There is nothing at all odd or queer about him.' Indeed, he seems to be 'a well-adjusted, happy person'.[17] He does not exhibit any signs of irrational thinking, delusions or nervousness, and appears to have normal emotions when talking about, for example, his family.

But beneath this 'mask of sanity' lurks a pathological mind, characterized by total insincerity: he 'shows a remarkable disregard for truth and is to be trusted no more in his accounts of the past than in his promises for the future or his statement of present intentions'. He can look at another person, the television camera or the court judge straight in the eye and tell a bold-faced lie. Not only will he retail untruths, making pledges he will never respect, but also he tends towards antisocial behaviour, including aggressive acts of violence, which will however produce no sense of shame or regret.[18] He has no emotional capacity for empathy, and thus can engage in killing even large numbers of innocent people without feeling remorse.

Although the penchant for lying is present in all the Arab figures considered here, most of them do not display such superficial signs of normality. The one exception is Bashar al-Assad, whose past record and behaviour during the Syrian protest movement deserve careful examination from this standpoint. Though, in response to the first protests, he promised reforms and the abolition of emergency rule, his regime simultaneously ordered security forces to open fire on demonstrators, raising the spectre of his father, who was responsible for up to 30,000 deaths in Hama in 1982.

When it comes to close personal relationships, personality disorders, especially narcissism, play a prominent role. If the narcissist finds a partner to his liking, he will not relate to that person as a love object – i.e. a separate person – but rather as someone who reflects his own ego as if s/he were an extension of his own self; consequently what was self-idealization becomes mutual idealization. Where narcissistic personalities come together in a partnership – as was the case of Slobodan Milošević and his wife Mila, for example, or Zine El-Abidine Ben Ali and his wife Leila Trabelsi – it often becomes a 'fortress marriage' in which 'mutually hostile impulses are redirected outwards against other people, groups or worldviews. The fortress marriage remains stable, despite its high conflict potential, because everything evil is to be perceived only outside and fought against there.' In many cases, it is the female partner who is the greater narcissist, and who ends up running affairs.[19]

Narcissists are *not* born; they are made, largely as a result of the type of family upbringing and broader cultural norms. A child who has an unhealthy relationship with mother and father – whereby either the parents break the will of the child or, conversely, the child controls the parents – may be a candidate for serious psychological problems.[20] In either case, the child will desire power for power's sake, to compensate for perceived injustice. In the case of Slobodan Milošević, a figure extensively scrutinized in psycho-historical studies, traumas in early childhood were decisive. When his father committed suicide, the young boy was thrust into the role of an adult who was expected to compensate his mother for the loss. His mother, an extremely overbearing person and political fanatic, also committed suicide, as did an uncle. Such traumatic events, if not overcome through profound mourning and worked through therapeutically, lead the individual to a sadomasochistic condition.

Children who have experienced such traumas tend to be 'loners' or 'ugly ducklings', without many school friends. Some are attracted to politics at an early age and seek gratification as would-be leaders to deal with their sense of loneliness and not being loved. Qaddafi used to stand up on a stool and repeat speeches by Nasser to impress his schoolmates. Such children often develop the ability to make up wild stories about adventures as a way of making themselves important and maintain this capability into adulthood. Most narcissists can become addicted to conscious lying. Other children may turn to narcissism as a means of compensating for an inferiority complex due to a real or perceived material or spiritual handicap. Coming from very humble beginnings may be enough to lead a child to compulsively seek a special place in society, as a means of redress for a state of poverty. One famous example of narcissism deriving from physical handicap is Napoleon Bonaparte, who developed a neurotic problem due to his slight stature.

The Leader and the Masses

If, for one reason or another, a political leader develops one or another severe personality disorder, this does not answer the question: why do masses of people not only accept him but worship him? Freud was the first to explore the dynamics of mass psychology and the relationship between the mass and the leader. Wirth sums up the concept as follows:

> In a psychological crowd, a common identification of all its members occurs both with each other and with their leader, onto whom they collectively project their own superego and ego ideals. Projecting their ego ideals and their superego on the leader frees the members of the crowd from confining norms, values and feelings of guilt so that they can act out their instinctive compulsions, their resentments originating in unconscious conflicts and their impulses toward aggression without being weighed down with self-reproach. In the leader's name, the crowd and also the individuals in it – to the extent that they have become integrated with the mass movement and therefore have surrendered their mental status as autonomous

individuals – are willingly carried away to perform impulse-driven actions, such as attacks, destruction and acts of violence which under normal circumstances, they would individually have refused to take part in.[21]

Historian and journalist Sead Husic has stressed the importance of collective trauma in shaping the willingness of a group, or even an entire population, to accept such a personality unconditionally. In the case of Serbia, it was the Ottomans' defeat of the Serbs in the Battle of the Kosovo Plain in 1389 that was the collective trauma. Instead of working through the trauma, successive generations transformed it into a myth, according to which, although they had lost the battle they had 'saved' Christianity from further advances. The event, celebrated in the national literature and music, had become the reference point for a sadomasochistic tendency: the people came to believe – and Milošević exploited the myth to the extreme – that, having suffered the defeat, they would have the right to prevail through revenge. Certain historical events in the Arab experience, from the Crusades to Ottoman oppression, from colonial subjugation to lost wars – especially the 1967 war –, hold a similar potential for shaping a culture of revenge, and the submission to a dictatorial leader believed to be capable of exacting it.

Even if an individual grows up in a healthy home and culture, and becomes an intelligent, conscientious, mature and moral political leader – possessing those qualities that Kernberg believes are prerequisites for leadership – wielding power itself can still have the effect of inducing narcissism.[22] As the saying goes, 'power corrupts'. Mario Erdheim writes: 'Even if one barred narcissists from access to power by means of a clever test, those individuals who did achieve power would sooner or later develop those characteristics' for the simple reason that it is 'power itself [...] that causes excessive narcissism.' Thus, as Erdheim summarizes it:

> The dilemma of ruling lies in that, on the one hand, it lays the foundations to promote human development through a better control of nature, but that, on the other hand, it impedes the societal acquirement of those prerequisites at the same time through the unleashing of narcissism, thus advancing the destruction of the culture to the development of which it had contributed.[23]

The question posed in this study, and which the reader must attempt to answer, is: are these leaders persons who, because of childhood traumas or other family or social influences, developed personality disorders? Or are they essentially healthy individuals who have been corrupted in the process of their serving in positions of leadership?

NOTES

1. Freud, Sigmund, 'Zur Einführung des Narzissmus', in *Gesammelte Werke, Zehnter Band, Werke aus den Jahren 1913–1917*, Imago Publishing Co., Ltd., London, 1949, Volume 10, pp. 137–170.
2. Spaas, Lieve (ed.), *Echoes of Narcissus*, Berghahn Books, New York, Oxford, 2000, pp. 1–2.
3. Kohut, H., *The Analysis of the Self: A Systematic Approach to the Psychoanalytic Treatment of Narcissistic Personality Disorders*, International Universities Press, Inc., New York, 1971, passim.
4. Kernberg, Otto F., 'Sanctioned Social Violence', in *International Journal of Psychoanalysis* 84 (2003), pp. 683–698, cited by Wirth, Hans-Jürgen, *Narcissism and Power: Psychoanalysis of Mental Disorders in Politics,* translation by Ingrid Lansford (*Narzissmus und Macht, Zur Psychoanalyse seelischer Störungen in der Politik*), Psychosozial-Verlag, Giessen, 2002, 2009, p. 64. See also Kernberg, *Aggression in Personality Disorders and Perversions*, Yale University Press, New Haven and London, 1992.
5. Ibid., pp. 66–67.
6. Ibid., pp. 34, 40.
7. Kohut, 'Thoughts on Narcissism and Narcissistic Rage', in *Psychoanalytic Study of the Child*, 27, pp. 365, cited in Wirth, op. cit., p. 40.
8. Wirth, ibid., pp. 62–63.
9. Kernberg, Otto F., *Aggression in Personality Disorders and Perversions*, op. cit., p. 67; Wirth, op. cit., pp. 145–147.
10. Kernberg, Otto F., *Ideologie, Konflikt und Führung: Psychoanalyse von Gruppenprozessen und Persönlichkeitsstruktur*, J.G. Cotta'sche Buchhandlung Nachfolger GmbH, Stuttgart, 2000, translation by Elisabeth Vorspohl, (*Ideology, Conflict, and Leadership in Groups and Organizations*, Yale University Press, New Haven, 1998), p. 171.
11. Wirth, op. cit., p. 67.
12. Riemann, Fritz, *Anxiety: Using Depth Psychology to Find a Balance in Your Life*, translation by Greta Dunn (*Grundformen der Angst: Eine tiefenpsychologische Studie*), Ernst Reinhardt Verlag, München, Basel, 2006, 2009). Psychiatrists differentiate between narcissistic or hysterical personality structures, and narcissistic or hysterical syndromes in various personality structures.
13. Ibid., p. 198.
14. Ibid., p. 195.
15. Ibid., p. 175.

16 Ibid., p. 198.
17 Cleckley, Hervey, M.D., *The Mask of Sanity: An Attempt to Clarify Some Issues About the So-Called Psychopathic Personality*, Literary Licensing, LLC, Whitefish, MT, 2011, p. 382.
18 Ibid., pp. 387, 389.
19 Husic, Sead, *Psychopathologie der Macht: Die Zerstörung Jugoslawiens im Spiegel der Biografien von Milošević, Tudjman und Izetbegović*, Verlag Hans Schiler, Berlin, 2007, pp. 34–35. This is also known as a 'symbiotic couple', Wirth, op. cit., p. 156.
20 Wirth, op. cit., pp. 81, 92.
21 Ibid., pp. 47–48, Freud, 'Massenpsychologie und Ich-Analyse', in *Gesammelte Werke*, op. cit., *Dreizehnter Band*, 1947, Volume 13, pp. 71–161.
22 Kernberg, 1998, 2000, p. 63.
23 Erdheim, M., *Die gesellschaftliche Produktion von Unbewusstheit. Eine Einführung in den ethnopsychoanalytischen Prozess*, Suhrkamp, Frankfurt, 1982, pp. 410–411, cited by Wirth, op. cit., p. 197.

2

Muammar Qaddafi: King of Kings

Sometime in mid-February 2011, when hundreds of thousands of Libyans were flooding city centres in demonstrations chanting that Colonel Qaddafi must step down, the Leader held a four-hour meeting with an Arab associate and dedicated 20 minutes of that conversation to raise what was evidently a burning issue for him at the time: where might he find a capable plastic surgeon who might give him a face-lift? Robert Fisk, a reliable journalist who reported the event in an article in the *Independent* on 22 February, swears that it 'is a true story'. There is no reason to doubt the veracity of the report. In fact, it stands out as a particularly apt symbol of Qaddafi's personality disorder.

Libya's dictator not only betrayed this and other symptoms of the narcissistic personality; he constituted perhaps the most complete textbook example of the pathology in the public realm. Qaddafi offered literally every syndrome identified by psychoanalysis as related to narcissism, hysteria and paranoia. In short, the man was seriously mentally ill, a fact that should have sufficed to warrant his departure from political power and placement under psychiatric care.

Long before the outbreak of the Libyan uprising, initially a peaceful protest which the regime transformed into civil war, prominent political figures worldwide had recognized neurotic, if not psychotic, attributes in the Libyan leader. He appeared to Nasser, who was Qaddafi's hero and role model, as 'a nice boy but terribly naive'.[1] Nasser related the humorous story of a shrimp dinner the two shared. Qaddafi, who had never seen a shrimp before in his life, asked, terrified: 'What are these? Locusts? Do you eat locusts in Egypt?' he wanted to know. Nasser reassured him that they were seafood called shrimps, and quite good to eat. Qaddafi's rejection was absolute: 'I can't eat fish,' he said, 'because it is not killed according to correct Muslim ritual with someone saying "*Allahu akbar*" at the moment of slaughter. These have just been allowed to die: I couldn't possibly eat them.'[2]

Nasser died only a year after Qaddafi's seizure of power, but his successor, Anwar Sadat, had ample opportunity to experience more than the young Libyan leader's naivety. In April 1975, when Qaddafi was spreading slanders against the Egyptian head of state, Sadat told a journalist from the Kuwaiti paper *Al-Siyasah:* 'Qaddafi is one hundred percent mad. A devil has entered into him and he imagines things that are not real.'[3] The Soviet leadership shared this view, and reportedly was exploring possibilities to replace him. One high level military official in Moscow was quoted in a CIA report calling Qaddafi a 'madman on top of a pile of gold [i.e. oil]',[4] while a Russian diplomat told an aide of Nasser's: 'He [Qaddafi] is crazy.'[5] For Chadian President Hissein Habré, whose country Qaddafi had tried to control, he was 'That disease called Qaddafi ...'[6] Ronald Reagan called him the 'mad dog of the Middle East' and former German President Christian Wulff depicted him as a 'psychopath'. The German weekly magazine *Der Spiegel* carried a feature on Qaddafi's psychological condition based on studies done by Professor Jerrold Post, from George Washington University, who had worked 21 years as a CIA profiler. In Post's view, Qaddafi was '[a] high-grade narcissistic leader ... obsessed with dreams of fame ...'[7]

None of these characterizations constitute libel. They are on the mark. Those who had doubted or underestimated the insanity of Qaddafi's behaviour could no longer close their eyes after the events that unfolded in February 2011. As German journalist and Middle East expert Ulrich Kienzle remarked at a meeting of the German–Arab Society in Berlin that month: 'At the very latest, when Qaddafi pulled the "umbrella trick", you had to recognize that the man is crazy.' He was referring to the scene broadcast on state television on 22 February showing the Libyan leader sitting inside a jeep-like vehicle resembling Benedict XVI's *papamobile*, with a huge beach-sized umbrella opened out in front of him. He told a reporter that he actually wanted to go down to the city centre to talk to the demonstrators, but, since it was raining, he decided against it.

Narcissistic Self-Aggrandizement

As the clinical literature emphasizes, the narcissist has an overblown estimation of his qualities and capabilities, and tends to advertise this loudly. After then-President Reagan ordered the bombing of Qaddafi's residence in 1986 in retaliation for the Berlin La Belle terror attack, the Libyan leader preserved the shelled ruins as a monument to his presumed invulnerability and, to underline the superpower's audacity, he commissioned a huge metal statue to be placed there in the shape of a fist mercilessly crushing an American plane.

One of his first televised addresses during the civil conflict was staged in front of the husk of this former residence. There, on 22 February 2011, he apotheosized the event: 'I am talking to you from the house which was bombarded by 170 planes by America and Britain. They left all houses and were aiming for Muammar's houses. Is it because he is president of the country? They could have treated him like other presidents, but Muammar Qaddafi is history, resistance, freedom, victory, revolution. This is a testimony from the highest authority that Muammar Qaddafi is not the president, he is not a normal person. You cannot poison him or lead demonstrations against him.' Then, implicitly addressing the opposition, he asked rhetorically: 'When bombs were falling on my house and killing my children, where were you, you rats? ... You were in America ... One hundred and seventy planes left all palaces and kings alone and came to the great house of Muammar Qaddafi. This is a victory that should not be relinquished by anybody, any country or people in Africa or any nation. Fighting back the tyranny of America, we did not give in, we were resilient.'

'Libya wants glory,' he announced. 'Libya wants to be at the pinnacle of the world. I am a fighter, a revolutionary from the tents.' He went on prophetically: 'I will die as a martyr in the end' after fighting 'to the last drop of my blood.' He ordered his fellow Libyans to mobilize: 'You men and women who love Qaddafi ... Get out of your homes and fill the streets. Leave your homes and attack them in their lairs. They are taking your children and getting them drunk and sending them to death. For what? To destroy Libya, burn Libya,' he claimed.

'Now is the time for action,' he exhorted his supporters. 'Now is the time for victory. No retreat! Forward!!!! Forward!!!! Revolution!' and, after pounding his fists frenetically on the table, stood up and left.

Qaddafi was unequivocal regarding the outcome of the conflict. He, Libya and his people would prevail. 'We can crush any enemy,' he told supporters in Green Square on 25 February. 'We can crush it with the people's will.' And, displaying a tendency characteristic of leaders afflicted with narcissism, he cast his people's ability to win in terms of their historic victories, in this case, over the Italians. 'These are the youth,' he said, 'the sons and grandsons of the martyrs of battles against the Italian invasion, the Italian Empire which was crushed by your fathers and grandfathers.'

In these remarks, Qaddafi also launched into a self-laudatory panegyric: 'If the Libyan people do not love me, then I do not deserve to live,' he said. 'If the Arab people, the African people, and all people, do not love Muammar Qaddafi, Muammar Qaddafi does not deserve life for one day! If my people do not love me, I do not deserve life for one day.' He concluded with an appeal to his followers to prepare for the coming confrontation in high spirits, indeed, in a celebratory mood: 'You must dance, sing and prepare yourself ... Dance, sing, rejoice!'

The themes developed in this address were to reappear in several subsequent statements and speeches. The central message was the narcissistic conviction that he would prevail against all odds in the ongoing conflict, as his country had prevailed earlier in history. Speaking to a select group of followers in Tripoli on 15 March he declared: 'Whatever the plot against us, we are going to stand against it. We are going to destroy them. The Libyan people should stand and fight the imperialist powers. We have defeated them before and we will defeat them another time. The Libyan people will be victorious, freedom will be victorious and Libyan Jumahariya will be victorious.' (His son, Saif, was just as categorical in an interview with the press that day, when he confidently announced that the battle would be over within 48 hours.) Dressed in his typical brown desert cape and pillbox hat, the leader then stood up and, pumping the air with raised fists, melted into the crowd.

On 17 March after launching air raids on Benghazi, Qaddafi delivered a speech, translated by AlJazeera, in which, according to press commentary, he equated himself with Allah, or with the Prophet Mohammed, in that he promised the rebels, 'those who have been forced to follow those infidels', that they would be forgiven, just as the Prophet had promised a follower who had erred, that Allah had forgiven him. This belief that he was God-like, a trait often encountered in narcissistic personalities, emerged with increasing frequency in Qaddafi's behaviour as the conflict escalated.

Qaddafi also met with the international press several times during the initial phase of the conflict and exploited each appearance as an opportunity to project his grandiose self as the universally beloved leader of his people, if not all people. But his behaviour betrayed his near-psychotic state. When a BBC reporter asked him what he planned to do about the rebellion, Qaddafi responded with an uncontrollable, hysterical laugh. He was visibly dissociated, and appeared to be about to unravel. After managing to pull himself together, he asked quite seriously: 'What is the question?' The BBC reporter rephrased it, saying there was a rebellion afoot and what was he as a leader prepared to do about it? The answer was extended mumbling and a long, low, loud groan. Then, evading the issue utterly, he elaborated on his respect for the press as an institution, evidently in an attempt to manipulate his interlocutor. The only thing of substance he could say was that those causing trouble were 'Al Qaida'.

Reality Knocks at the Door

What happens when that entity feared by all narcissists – reality – suddenly appears on the stage of political events? Reality asserted itself in Libya with the first opposition manifestations but Qaddafi blocked that psychologically with his self-serving rationalization that it was all a plot by outside forces, and that Al Qaida was at work.

However, on 17 March, when the United Nations Security Council voted up a resolution of questionable legality which called for a no-fly zone over Libya and specified that 'all necessary measures' would be allowed to protect Libyan citizens from military attacks by government forces, Muammar Qaddafi found himself in a new universe and a completely novel psychological context. He was suddenly confronted by reality with a capital R.

What could he do? One possibility would have been to take flight – not into exile (something such a grandiose self could never live with) – but into death. Qaddafi had, after all, repeatedly asserted his willingness to fight to the end, preferring a martyr's death on Libyan soil to any other option.

The alternative would be to make a deal, something that, from a pragmatic, political standpoint, would be the most rational choice. Rumours had already circulated that the US and European governments had been canvassing African governments in search of a country which would offer him refuge.

Qaddafi's response came in a lengthy speech made on 29 April, in which he reiterated his commitment to resist, yet indicated willingness to negotiate under certain conditions. His opening remarks were clinically significant: 'We provided you with all the means to get you out of this predicament you are in,' he told his international interlocutors in a fantasy-moulded reversal of roles. 'You are facing people who are insisting on death,' he said, 'Freedom or death.' Whether aware of it or not, Qaddafi was aping the slogans of the rebels, who had, by that time, already suffered an estimated 10,000 dead and showed no signs of capitulating. The Libyan leader was adamant: 'We will not surrender. We will not leave. We will not go into exile.'

Yet, reality *had* provoked a shock even on this deranged mind. Abandoning his earlier characterization of the Security Council as a 'Mickey Mouse council', Qaddafi said the body 'must convene' in this case, since 'there is an aggression on a country, a war between two countries', and the Security Council's mandate therefore demands that it intervene, although not – he specified – to determine the internal affairs of his country. The most remarkable statement made by Qaddafi followed: 'In any case, we are now facing reality,' he said. 'Let us negotiate. What do you want?' He expressed his readiness to negotiate with France, Britain, Italy, the US as well as NATO and the European Union. 'Let us negotiate with you,' he pleaded, 'the countries that attack us. Let us negotiate.' And he added: 'Why are you attacking us?'

Mouthing such words must have been painful for Qaddafi, as evidenced in the fact that he often read from a prepared text when speaking of negotiations, nervously shuffling the papers while reading. He devoted a significant amount of time in his speech to expressing his gratitude to the people of Abu Saleem, who had offered him the headquarters of the General People's Committee after his own headquarters had been obliterated by NATO aerial bombardments. Here he was indirectly appealing to other tribes and cities to join his forces in resisting.

He concluded his agitated speech with quotes from the Qur'an, in which Allah asserted that when all act together, they will achieve victory. Gesticulating with his index finger, Qaddafi applied this to the immediate situation, saying: 'The NATO will be defeated. Soon will their multitude be made to fight and they will show their backs.' Clapping both hands loudly on the table, the leader then rose and left.

As the NATO attacks escalated, targeting Qaddafi's residences and reportedly killing family members, he disappeared from public view. Contrary to his earlier assertion, Qaddafi was not facing reality but trying to escape it. And in the real world of power politics, pressures were mounting on him. The International Criminal Court (ICC) announced an arrest warrant against him, his son Saif, and his brother-in-law and intelligence chief Abdulla al Senussi for crimes against humanity on 16 May. By that time, NATO war planes engaged in the 'Unified Protector' operation facilitated by UN Resolution 1973 had run more than 10,000 devastating sorties.

Unconfirmed press reports in mid-May spoke of Italian initiatives to find an 'honorable exit' for the Libyan leader, exile in some friendly country, and Russian President Dmitry Medvedev later offered in a G-8 meeting to mediate. The African Union also prepared a ceasefire initiative for Qaddafi and perhaps exile, but it came to nothing. Rebel sources told *Asharq Al-Awsat* on 28 May that the National Transitional Council leader Mustafa Abdul Jalil had said the NTC 'could pledge not to legally pursue any Libyan official, including Qaddafi, on condition that he leave the country with his family and his top aides, to reside in one of the African states that is not a signatory' to the ICC. The official speaker of Qaddafi's government Moussa Ibrahim reiterated that exile and resignation were not options. As Saif al Qaddafi had repeatedly insisted, his father and he would live in Libya and die in Libya.

On 31 May it was reported that five generals and three other senior officers surfaced in Rome and appealed to their colleagues to join them in the opposition, something 120 other officers had already done. British source reports had it in late May that Qaddafi's paranoia had reached such heights that he had gone into hiding in the capital, changing his whereabouts constantly, and often spending nights in hospitals. The Libyan leader was at the end of his rope.

In a speech delivered from a hideout on 7 June, Qaddafi waxed defiant. While his capital was being bombed mercilessly, he challenged 'the gutless', saying that Tripoli had been attacked many times in history, by Byzantium, the Romans, the Maltese, the Italians, but would continue to resist. 'We will not give up,' he promised. 'We have only one choice, which is to stay in Libya and either live or die. We will not surrender. You [NATO] are bastards; you have to leave, not us.'

By this time, reports had it that Qaddafi controlled only the army. International pressure was mounting for him to resign; Turkish Prime Minister Tayyip Erdogan offered him security guarantees if he left the country, but got no answer. Instead, on 13 June, Libyan national television broadcast footage of the Leader showing him in an undisclosed location playing chess with Kirsan Ilyumzhinov, visiting from Russia.

Ilyumzhinov is a businessman and former leader of the Buddhist republic of Kalmykia, who reportedly believed he had been taken on a spaceship tour by aliens. Qaddafi, responding to calls for his resignation, told his guest: 'I am neither premier nor president nor king. I do not hold any post in Libya and therefore I have no position which I should give up.'

Forced into hiding, Qaddafi addressed world public opinion during the escalating conflict via audio messages broadcast on state media. The message was unrelenting: on 17 June, he vowed he would stay in Libya and defeat NATO. Five days later, he reiterated his commitment to stay and resist, challenging NATO to 'strike with your missiles, two, three, 10 or 100 years'. In an audio message delivered on the night of 23 August, Qaddafi swore his forces would drive out the 'rats' who had entered the capital Tripoli and taken over his headquarters. He explained he had left his headquarters 'out of tactical considerations' because NATO destroyed it, and pledged he would fight to victory or die a martyr.

A peaceful solution could perhaps have been found, had the mediation efforts of the AU, the Italians or the Turks, among others, been allowed to continue, had Qaddafi *et al.* not signalled such intransigence and had the international forces behind the NATO war not been intent on total victory, sealed by Qaddafi's death. By the end of August, the NTC had reportedly promised that anyone who captured or killed Qaddafi would not be legally prosecuted, and a leading Libyan businessman put up a US$1.5 million bounty for his assassin. At the same time, reports were already circulating in *The Daily Telegraph* that special British units were hunting down Qaddafi and his family. The dictator's wife Safia, his daughter Aisha and two sons, Hannibal and Mohammed, managed to enter Algeria on 29 August, where they found refuge.

But Qaddafi, true to his pledge, died a martyr. The circumstances surrounding the identification of his hideout in Sirte, the aerial pursuit of his convoy as it attempted to flee and the armed conflict which led to his death on 20 October were clouded in mystery. According to composite accounts, it appears that Qaddafi left his bunker in Sirte together with close aides and bodyguards in a convoy headed west in the direction of Misratah. An American drone sighted the convoy and a French fighter jet bombed it, after which the various 75 vehicles scrambled in different directions. Twenty vehicles, one of them carrying Qaddafi, headed south but were hit by NATO bombs. Qaddafi, injured, crawled out of his vehicle and hid in a large water pipe. When apprehended, he and/or his aides said they would surrender, but were fired upon. In the ensuing shootout, Qaddafi was further wounded, then transported to an ambulance and, as the official story goes, died *en route*, as a result of his wounds. An autopsy later determined he had been shot at close range in the head and stomach. Whatever the details, it appears certain that he was summarily executed, together with his son Mutassim, then put on grotesque display for days in Misratah, in violation of any norm of human dignity and in contravention of Islamic tradition, which requires burial within 24 hours.

If published reports of his last moments have any credibility, Qaddafi, even at that juncture, did not grasp what was happening. One account says he came out of the water pipe asking, 'What's going on? Don't shoot!' The Saudi newspaper *Asharq Al-Awsat* quoted him asking his assailants: 'My children, you shoot me? I am Qaddafi, I am the Leader, why shoot?'

The Names of the Leader

Over the years Qaddafi had adopted a number of titles that provide insight into how he viewed his grandiose self. Once merely Leader of the Revolution and Brother Muammar, he later assumed the position of 'King of Kings of (North) Africa' and the 'dean of Arab Kings and presidents'.[8] In 1991, to deal with the Takfir wal-Hijrah movement (one of many opposition groups), Qaddafi arrogated to himself the authority of 'the Muslim Imam Muammar Qaddafi' and 'leader of the World Islamic Popular Leadership' to issue a fatwa declaring the group heretical. Without assuming any new titles, he announced in speeches in February and July 1978, that the Hijra calendar had to be revised, a move that brought the wrath of Saudi theologians down upon him.[9] In June 1986, this time playing emperor, he ordered a change in the names of the months of the year, but, since it was confined to Libya, no religious or political strife ensued.[10] Paradoxically, as noted, during the revolution Qaddafi insisted that he held no titles at all; in fact, because of this he could not 'resign from office', since he did not occupy any. It was the people who held power, not he.[11]

Such formal titles and presumed honours function as displays of extreme self-love. And if he, Qaddafi, were deserving of such love from himself, then should not others also express the same emotions? Qaddafi was convinced that this was the case. Speaking on television following the 1986 bombing raid, he claimed that, despite Washington's attempt to eliminate him, the people of the US actually adored him. As proof, he said an American woman had called him beforehand to forewarn him. On another occasion, he bragged that he had received lots of mail from American women who admired his good looks. 'They often say they like my hair,' he explained.[12]

A personality who is so convinced of his extraordinary qualities will strive to show them off in the form of exhibitionism. Most obvious in Qaddafi was his extravagant, if not gaudy, attire ranging across many garish colours. Visitors report that he often changed his clothes several times a day and was very aware of his trend-setting reputation in fashion.[13]

Such a self-important individual demands preferential handling by others, and makes quite sure that they comply. When travelling abroad on official visits, Qaddafi insisted on residing with his extravagant entourage in his enormous Bedouin tent, and took along with him a couple of camels especially flown in to provide him fresh milk daily. (Whether by coincidence or not, King Idriss, whom Qaddafi overthrew in his 1969 coup, was also known to drink camel milk at all times.)[14] In the human part of his entourage were his fabled female bodyguards, up to 40 in number, and reputedly all virgins,[15] as well as a Ukrainian nurse, Galyna Kolotnyzka (who asked for political exile in Norway in May 2011). According to other sources, at one time he had a nurse and masseuse from Yugoslavia and a third woman from East Germany. When visiting his good friend Silvio Berlusconi in Rome, Qaddafi reportedly made sure there were about 100 girls between the ages of 18 and 35, all 1.7 metres (or more) tall, on hand. When the girls arrived, he would launch into a lecture on the Holy Qur'an.[16] In contrast, there are also a number of accounts pointing to somewhat less platonic relations with women, which range from flirtation to outright sexual advances.[17]

Muammar, the Malignant Narcissist

Like many other dictators, Qaddafi combined the features of narcissism together with extreme paranoia. In this case, according to the psychoanalytical literature, 'malignant narcissism' develops, character-ized by black-and-white thinking in friend/enemy categories. Enemies are treated with the greatest contempt and subjected to brutal repression, even to the point of physical elimination.

For Qaddafi, all opposition groups, whether the Muslim Brotherhood, Takfir wal-Hijra or others, were agents of the enemy. 'We are on one side,' he said in a 1991 speech, 'and imperialism, America, Zionism, Europe, calls for humbug, heresy, assassins, murder perpetrators, knife users and the humbug people are all on the other side.' Such wretched beings deserve only words of abuse. 'All these people, these sons of bitches I am telling you about, are sent by the enemies of religion and the enemies of the Arab nation from abroad to sabotage religion ...'[18]

Once the rebellion had broken out in Libya in 2011, the regime blamed Israeli intelligence (Mossad) and the US as instigators. Those engaged in the uprising were 'rats', 'greasy rats', a 'group of young people, who were given hallucinogenic pills' by Al Qaida, youth that was 'emulating what is happening in Tunisia', stated Qaddafi on 22 February. In his 15 March remarks to supporters, he called the opposition 'renegades and gangsters', 'rats and traitors'.

Thus, according to this mindset, it was not only justified but imperative to deploy brute force against them. In the same 22 February speech he vowed to mete out capital punishment to 'any Libyan who lifts an arm'. He explicitly referenced the massacre of Tiananmen Square, where 'those who were in front were crushed to death [by the tanks]. And whoever died, the unity of China is more important than those people in the square ...' And Qaddafi did indeed target his own people, launching aerial bombardments which were used to justify international intervention. It was after he issued the credible threat that he would bomb and invade Benghazi and 'show no mercy', that the UN passed its resolution to erect a no-fly zone.

The sadistic cruelty of his offensive against the opposition knew no bounds. On 19 February, security units opened fire on a funeral party made up of Libyan citizens who had gathered to bury those who had been killed by government troops, and a massacre ensued. On 4 March, photographs reached the press showing 20 men who had been killed by government troops. Their hands had been tied behind their backs, and they were summarily executed because they refused to fight with Qaddafi's forces. That same day, a Friday, up to one hundred young people were 'disappeared' prior to a demonstration.

US Defense Secretary Robert Gates cited intelligence reports 'about Qaddafi taking the bodies of the people he's killed and putting them at the sites where we've attacked'. This was to prop up Libyan claims that the coalition air strikes were killing civilians. Opposition sources reported that once Qaddafi's troops had taken a town, they would dig up the graves of rebels to eliminate evidence of mass killings.

On 2 April, his tanks opened fire on homes and inhabited areas of Misratah, a fiercely contested site. As reported in the German press on 1 April, regime soldiers captured by the opposition said that two weeks earlier Qaddafi had personally ordered the total destruction of Benghazi, the opposition's stronghold. He had said that he would visit the city only if and when he, from outside the city gates, were able to gaze across the remains of the city and sight a fishing village on the eastern side, i.e. only after the entire city had been obliterated.

Foreign journalists were preferred targets, since Qaddafi believed they were deployed by the enemy (the US and Israel) to spread lies about the situation. Jürgen Todenhöfer, a former German political figure and journalist, published his first-hand account of how Qaddafi's forces homed in on his vehicle. His friend and guide Abdul Latif was incinerated when the vehicle was hit by surface-to-surface missiles, perhaps carrying napalm or phosphorus. For hours afterwards he and his associates, who had left the vehicle in time, were subjected to missile and grenade attacks.

On 17 April, Human Rights Watch reported that Libyan government forces were dropping cluster bombs on the besieged city of Misratah, hitting the hospital among other targets, and sending residents into panicked flight. US Secretary of State Hillary Clinton repeated the charge a few days thereafter. In late May, Qaddafi ordered the deployment of anti-personnel bombs and had mines laid in the Misratah harbour to prevent humanitarian aid from arriving at the besieged city by ship.

This was not the first time that the regime had preached and practised cruel aggression against its own citizens. As long ago as the beginning of August 1991, Qaddafi delivered a speech to elementary school children in their ninth class. After admonishing them to avoid evil and to do good, he unveiled a list of those who 'had failed': the Palestinians, who had 'failed' to liberate Jerusalem; and 'a generation from which came the agents, the stray dogs, the mercenaries, the deserters and all the scum who are eating the leftovers of the Americans and the English ...' The term 'stray dogs' refers to Libyan opposition members abroad, those who were systematically sought out and eliminated by Libyan hit squads over decades. Qaddafi went on to tell his audience of tender age that he and his regime would kill all such opponents. 'We are determined,' he said, 'to liquidate anyone suffering from this disease [opposition] because this disease is infectious; it means that this disease recruits any one of us and places him on the enemy's side. If you from now on find anyone in your own front has been recruited by the enemy, then you should immediately execute him in front of the people. This has always been done in any era.'

'We are determined,' Qaddafi concluded, 'to carry out the physical liquidation of anyone joining these movements because these movements subvert Islam and pan-Arabism and destroy our ranks and serve the enemy. [Audience shouts slogans: We are ready and have resolved to fight; on a signal from you, O Muammar, the Sixth Fleet will be destroyed.]'[19]

Killing of individuals as well as on a mass scale continued throughout the years. In 1993, following an aborted coup mounted by the Warfalla tribe, the father of one of the coup plotters went to the authorities to ask about the imminent release of his son from jail. The security forces beat him so badly that he died of his wounds. Later, they sought to dig up his remains, and cast them into the sea.[20] In 1996, in response to a prison riot, Qaddafi ordered his forces to open fire and 1,200 inmates were gunned down in cold blood. The list of gruesome acts perpetrated by Qaddafi would fill more than the pages of this book.

So much for dealing with the enemy on Libyan soil. To deal with the external enemy, Qaddafi had for decades financed, equipped, and politically supported virtually every terrorist outfit on the map. Israeli intelligence reported in 1986 that Qaddafi provided logistical, political and/or financial support to an estimated fifty terrorist groups, as well as the Palestinian rejectionists (PFLP, PFLP-GC, Abu Nidal, the Democratic Front, etc.), the Armenian terrorist ASALA, the Basque separatist ETA, the Irish IRA, the German Baader-Meinhof, Italian Red Brigades and subversive organizations in Latin America and Asia.[21]

His direct agents were responsible for signal hits, like the 1986 bombing of the La Belle discotheque in Berlin, the 1984 assassination of British policewoman Yvonne Fletcher in London, killed by a marksman shooting from the Libyan Embassy, the 1988 Lockerbie explosion of a plane which left a total 270 dead. In August 2003 Qaddafi assumed responsibility for that attack (although many questions remain open regarding the event), paid compensation to families of victims and thereby acquired readmission into the 'international community'. At about the same time, Qaddafi made a bombastic declaration that he was renouncing production of weapons of mass destruction, including nuclear weapons – weapons that he probably did not possess!

Delusions of Grandeur

Qaddafi always nurtured the illusion not only that he would be invulnerable to attacks from his multiple enemies at home and abroad, but also that he would ultimately be in a position to determine the course of historical events. His reasoning was that, since he, Qaddafi, was who he was, he had the right and the power to issue orders that must be fulfilled as a matter of course. This is a good illustration of the narcissist's illusion of being God-like. Thus he had the right to determine who should live and who should die. On the 24th anniversary of the founding of the state of Israel, a group of American Jews had chartered *Queen Elizabeth II* for a cruise to Ashdod. Qaddafi summoned the commander of an Egyptian submarine and asked if he could identify the ship. When he got an affirmative answer, he ordered him to aim two torpedoes at it and sink it.[22] Reportedly, in the autumn of 1982, Qaddafi told Aziz Sherib (the secretary of Libya's embassy in Jordan): 'I want you to arrange the assassination of King Hussein.' His idea was apparently to target the Jordanian king's plane with a surface-to-air missile.[23] He also developed plans to assassinate the US Ambassador in Cairo Herman Eilts. In 1983, Tripoli radio issued a call for the assassination of Mubarak.[24] Nothing came of these threats and plots, but they aptly depict his state of mind.

In this context, money assumes a special role, because such exploits are not cheap. The narcissist often believes money can buy anything. After learning from Nasser that Israel had a nuclear capability which the Arabs lacked, Qaddafi decided Libya had to acquire such a capability. He dispatched his aide Major Abdul Salam Jalloud to Cairo to tell the Egyptian leader that he thought the Chinese might be open to selling nuclear bombs, then to Peking for the purchase. The Chinese Premier Chou en-Lai informed Jalloud that they were not in the business of supplying nuclear weapons and it ended there.[25] The assumption behind the offer to purchase nuclear weapons was of course that the Chinese would be willing to make a sale, for profit. Qaddafi had offered Sudan US$3 billion if it would cut ties to the US and pledged US$5 billion to Egypt if it tore up the Camp David accord.[26] In the 2011 revolution it was regime funds that bought black African mercenaries, as well as Libyans. The Libyan leader reportedly paid family members of those who had died in the conflict around US$190,000 and set a bounty on the head of the opposition of US$400,000.[27]

Magic also played an important role. It was reported that the murdered leader had kept a small pouch with him filled with amulets. According to Colonel Saleh Mansour al-Obeidi, who defected to join the rebellion, Qaddafi had turned to African magicians, from Morocco, Nigeria, Gambia and Mauritania for aid in combating the revolution. As reported in *Asharq Al-Awsat* on 1 July, al-Obeidi thought Qaddafi considered magic to be like an auxiliary intelligence tool through which he could spy on enemies. A Qaddafi aide who confided in al-Obeidi reported that Qaddafi engaged a Gambian witch who used talismans and voodoo to protect the leader. The aide reported that: 'This witch has provided Qaddafi with a magic talisman which he wears on his cloak so that he is not hit by bullets or hurt in an explosion ... and this is why we always see him wearing this cloak.' Al-Obeidi also pointed to photographs of Qaddafi showing him wearing a ring made of hyena bone, given to him by a Mauritanian magician to ward off evil influences.

Nothing but Untruths

Narcissistic personalities are prone to lying, even from early childhood. This serves not only as a means of self-aggrandizement, but also expresses again a God-like illusion, according to which, 'if I say so, it must be true'. Thus, when confronted with an international confiscation of his assets in foreign banks and institutions, Qaddafi lied: 'I have no money abroad. You have no trace of any proof.'[28] While preparing an assault on Benghazi, Qaddafi's army issued a statement to the city's citizens to the effect that they were on a 'humanitarian mission' to save the populace from terrorists. Mussa Kussa, while still Qaddafi's foreign minister, announced a ceasefire, because the Qaddafi regime 'has great interest in protecting civilians'.[29] The official press agency Jana had, in fact, reported that the army would halt all hostile actions to allow the rebels to give up their weapons. Qaddafi stated that the reason he had sent his son al-Saadi to Benghazi was to 'implement an action plan for the improvement of infrastructure'. Shortly thereafter, he threatened to 'force the traitors out of Benghazi' and show no mercy. The government's offer of a ceasefire was repeated several times during the civil war, every time without consequence.

In a series of exchanges with the foreign press, he retailed one lie after another about the situation. On 27 February, in a telephone interview with the Serbian television station Pink TV – arranged by former Milošević intimate Zoran Lilic – he claimed: 'The country is under control, the only problem are the armed gangs that control Al Qaida [sic: that are controlled by Al Qaida].' He went on to elaborate: 'First of all there are no incidents at the moment, and Libya is entirely peaceful. There is nothing unusual, no riots.' He retailed the same line in a meeting with journalists from BBC and ABC in a Tripoli hotel. When journalist Christiane Amanpour asked him about the protests, he denied everything. 'No demonstrations at all in the streets,' he announced. 'No, no one against us. Against me, for what? I am not president. They love me, all my people with me, they love me all. They will die to protect me, my people.' When pressed on the uprising centred in Benghazi, he snarled: 'Al Qaida, [it] is Al Qaida, not my people.' On 15 March, he told N-TV in an interview that reports of his having repressed peaceful demonstrators were 'lies'. There had been 'only 150 to 200 dead,' he said, 'and the half of them were security forces. They died when police stations were stormed.'

It has been mooted that Qaddafi also lied about the fate of his own kin in the 1986 US aerial bombardments. The story that the press heard after the fact was that an adopted daughter Hanna had perished. But prior to the event, no mention had been made of such an adopted child, and her age was variously given as 12 months or five years.

Another tell-tale sign of psychological disorder appeared in Qaddafi's repeated projections of his own mental problems onto others. Thus, when the vote was cast at the UN Security Council for action against Libya, he pronounced French President Nicolas Sarkozy to be 'psychologically disturbed', and termed the opposition's ceasefire proposals as 'mad'.

Like Father, like Son ... and Daughter
Qaddafi's son, Saif al-Islam al-Qaddafi, who regularly filled in for his father at press meetings, presented the same arrogant demeanour and

propensity to lie. Speaking to ABC on 28 February 2011, he asserted that the entire country was 'calm', that the government 'didn't use force', and challenged his interviewer, 'show me a single bomb'. Asked what would happen were his father to leave the country, he stated: 'There would be war, civil war in Libya.' As for family assets abroad having been frozen, he lied that the family was 'very modest' and had no foreign bank accounts. He blithely denied that any leading Libyan had defected. In a second interview with the same American station on 17 March, when UN action was being prepared, Saif again rejected claims that there had been any air attacks against civilians. 'Have we seen a single civilian casualty?' he asked rhetorically. 'So there was no bloodshed in Libya.'

Contrary to his insistence that his father would live and die on Libyan soil, it was reported that Saif had sent an emissary to London in early April to explore possible scenarios for him to take over, leaving Qaddafi with a merely symbolical role. *Asharq Al-Awsat* cited Libyan 'sources' to the effect that the senior Qaddafi would perhaps accept such a compromise, but when asked by Reuters, Saif dismissed such a notion as 'ridiculous' and proceeded to elaborate on his plans for vast reforms, a new constitution, elections and so forth. In subsequent interviews, Saif went on like a broken record. Speaking to the *Washington Post* on 17 April, he compared the reports of civilian casualties, which had been exploited to justify UN action for a free-fly zone, to lies about Iraq's weapons of mass destruction before the last war. He swore that if anyone were shot in Tripoli, the numbers were low. 'One, two, three, 10 people, 20, 30, maybe, maybe nobody knows, maybe by accident, but first, there was no intention. Second, people are talking about hundreds and thousands. There is a big difference between two or three and two or three thousand,' he concluded. This time, when queried about the consequences of his father's possible departure, he answered: 'Somalia, Part two. Everybody knows that.'

Saif's sister Aisha proved to be made of the same cloth as father and brother in her public remarks from Tripoli in mid-April. She denounced calls for Qaddafi's resignation as a provocation that insulted every Libyan. Her father, she said, was not only in Libya, but lived in the heart of every Libyan. Ergo: 'Whoever does not want Qaddafi does not deserve to live.' In those days, Tripoli supporters were chanting, 'Only Allah, Muammar and Libya.'

After Qaddafi had gone into hiding, this changed. Aisha fled with her mother and two brothers to Algeria on 29 August, where she gave birth to a child the following day. Saif went underground and, after reports circulated at the end of August that he had been captured, he resurfaced, laughing and cheering in front of cameras. In late October, after his father's death, again rumours suggested that he had been arrested or killed. At the same time, he may have been in discreet negotiations with the ICC to surrender rather than die. On 19 November, he was finally arrested in the southern desert with three companions and handed over to the newly formed government, to be tried either in Libya or by the ICC, or both. Photographs of him dressed in desert robes and staring, dazed, into the camera like a deer caught in the headlights of a car circulated on the Internet.

Muammar Who?

If one is to understand the Qaddafi phenomenon, one must not only interpret his actions, speeches and so forth, but also examine his childhood and early years. Again, here we find a textbook example of the factors contributing to the development of a narcissistic personality.

The future revolutionary was born in September 1942 in a tent, the last of four children, and the only male. There were no doctors, no nurses, no midwives on hand.[30] His Bedouin parents lived in a tent, devoid of sanitary facilities or electricity, and would move periodically together with members of their extended family of 60 or so people from place to place in search of water and fodder for their animals. The head of the family, Mohammed Abdul Salam bin Hamed bin Mohammed, kept his camels, goats, ewes and rams. Not only was life in the desert difficult for a child of nomads, but also political events in the years of his infancy were dramatic and traumatic. He was still an infant when the battle of Alamein broke out, during which the British under Field Marshal Montgomery defeated Rommel's German forces. The Bedouins had no choice but to flee the hostilities. But they could not be spared the horrors of war, and had to walk by dead bodies and body parts strewn about, carrion for jackals.[31]

Qaddafi himself recounted his earliest traumatic memories. 'We were under fire and dodging bullets in the middle of the Second World War. Countries were fighting over our land. We had no idea why. Planes were flying over our land. Bombs were falling. Mines were exploding all over the place. We did not understand the reason why. *Those were my earliest childhood memories.*'[32]

Muammar 'from an early age ... appeared to be different from other children. He was serious, even taciturn ...' and 'seldom played with his cousins; rather he was always lost in thought about one thing or another'.[33] His father remarked that he was so withdrawn that he would respond only if directly addressed with a question. A schoolteacher said he was intelligent and pious, almost to the point of becoming ascetic. As a youth, he was fascinated by tales that his father or his Qur'an teacher would tell him of past exploits of his tribe and people. One story he wanted to hear again and again was about his grandfather's fight to the death against the Italians, and his father's own military experience after the First World War.[34] Omar Mukhtar, the leader of the Libyan resistance against the Italians, who fell in battle in 1931, was Qaddafi's hero. His Qur'an teacher, whom his illiterate father had engaged when Qaddafi was seven, told the boy stories about the Grand Senussi, who founded a Sufi order and unified many Libyan tribes.[35]

Muammar attended elementary school in Sirte, about 30 kilometres distant from his family tent. During the school week, he would live in Sirte and, for lack of financial means, would sleep in the mosque, then on Thursday walk home for the short weekend. He started secondary school at the age of fourteen in Sabha, where his family had moved to. It was there that he turned to politics.

Those were the years of the early Egyptian republic following Nasser's 1952 coup, as well as the rise of the Algerian liberation movement. Qaddafi set up the first clandestine cells with schoolmates there, among them Abdul Salam Jalloud, who was to remain a life-long close associate. Qaddafi would listen in rapt attention to Nasser's speeches beamed into Libya from Egypt, and studied his book *Philosophy of the Revolution*. He would memorize Nasser's speeches and recite them word for word for his contemporaries, standing on a small stool that served as a soapbox. In Mohamed Heikal's view, though he had memorized a lot, he understood little.[36] One of his teachers remembered that Qaddafi asked him quite openly how to organize a pyramid structure for a revolution against King Idriss, the notoriously corrupt monarch who had caved in to foreign demands for military bases.

Qaddafi's revolutionary rhetoric and political organizing got him in trouble. In October 1961 he rallied his classmates to a pro-Nasser demonstration denouncing the presence of foreign military bases in his own country. This earned him expulsion from school, but probably a good deal of admiration from his contemporaries, reinforcing his overblown estimates of his own worth.

His formal military training took place at the Royal Military Academy in Benghazi, touted as the Libyan Sandhurst. Qaddafi himself related: 'When we decided to go to the Military Academy, it was not because we wanted to become professional soldiers but because we wanted to infiltrate the institution and prepare for revolution.' He lamented the fact that Libya was 'occupied by foreign forces' – there were US and Italians, along with British bases, in the country. 'It was our duty', he said, 'to liberate our country from this occupation.'[37]

Colonel Ted Lough, who led the British Military Mission between 1960 and 1966, considered Qaddafi as 'our most backward cadet', who had failed exams and refused to learn English. Lough not only disliked Qaddafi, but also believed him to be 'inherently cruel', and suspected that he was responsible for killing a fellow cadet as well as the commander of the Academy in 1963. Another officer who disliked Qaddafi, Major Jalal Dalgeli, meted out a particularly sadistic form of punishment to him for insolence: with a heavy rucksack on his back, he was forced to get down on all fours and crawl on gravel in blistering heat, 'until the skin came off his knees'.[38]

Although such harsh treatment was not unusual in those institutions, it is easy to see how this could fuel the rage in the mind of a young man who had been severely traumatized as an infant in war, subjected to continuous bombing raids and to scenes of death and dying. The same young man had been raised on stories about the evil foreigners against whom his ancestors had fought to the death, and developed fantasies about taking on the hated outsiders in revenge.

Qaddafi was to have the opportunity to live out those fantasies in the coup against King Idriss, which he led in 1969. He set up his first cells while at school in Misratah, and imposed strict discipline on his co-conspirators. In 1964 the central committee of what was to become the Free Officers' Movement began its regular meetings and recruitment. In 1966, Qaddafi managed to attend a four-month training course at the Royal Armoured Corps headquarters in Dorset, although he reportedly hated Britain and the British.[39] It is curious, in this context, to note that Lough had reported his suspicions about Qaddafi's violence to British intelligence, which had him on file; yet he was allowed to travel to Britain for the training.

The Other Foreigners

For all his hatred of the Italians as oppressors, Qaddafi actually benefited from the services of the Mediterranean neighbour. It turns out that the Italian secret services were very much involved in the coup. Giovanni Fasanella, an Italian journalist and author who has written about the event, summarized it recently in an interview for *Cadoinpiedi*.[40] The 1969 coup 'had been organized in a hotel in Abano Terme in Veneto, by the Italian secret service. Qaddafi was our creature, having studied in Italian military academies'. Fasanella added that the Italians had saved Qaddafi's life at least twice, 'the first before the coup'. The English, he explained, 'who were angry because the colonel had expelled their military bases in Libya, had organized a military expedition with paid mercenaries and equipped a ship to send to the Libyan coast'. The mercenaries' task was to liberate anti-Qaddafi prisoners for a revolt against him. But the Italian secret services 'intercepted the ship in the port of Trieste and informed Qaddafi'. On another occasion, the Italians forewarned Qaddafi of a French plot to shoot down his plane.

Qaddafi was not the only person organizing a coup. Libyan Prime Minister Bakoush was one among about four figures who were mobilizing different groups of officers and intellectuals against the weak and corrupt King Idriss. Bakoush later claimed to have informed both the Americans and the King about Qaddafi's coup plans, and said that Washington had its own links to the plotters. Bakoush's theory is that the US, fearing a coup by more competent officers who were more politically allied to Nasser, chose to support Qaddafi in hopes of controlling him.[41]

Once in power, Qaddafi did enjoy the *de facto* support of the Americans. As leaked in a recent Italian periodical, the US State Department issued a memo dated 10 September 1969 which referenced Qaddafi's 'reluctance to be cooperative' with the US, but concluded that he 'is very close to being an indispensable man in the Libyan Arab Republic. If he were to disappear from the political stage, with all probability a period of instability would ensue.' In a document dated

20 September 1971, a follow-up text read: 'Qaddafi is the philosopher, the charismatic mobilizer of men and the driving force that pushes the Libyan revolution from one initiative to the next, in particular in the realm of foreign policy.'[42]

How the bloodless coup took place on 1 September 1969 is history. It was soon to become the stuff of mythology for Colonel Qaddafi, whose claim to fame rested on this achievement. In his first proclamation to the people in the name of the Revolutionary Command Council, he lauded the will of the people and the prowess of the army:

> Great people of Libya! In response to your iron will for self-determination; in fulfilment of your precious aspirations; in answer to your incessant call for change and purification; heeding your urging to action and to initiative, to revolution and decisive action, your armed forces have accomplished the overthrow of a reactionary, backward and rotten regime – whose stench once disgusted us, and the sight of whose corrupt machinations caused our hair to stand on end. Thus, with one stroke from your heroic army, idols fell and were destroyed. In one fatal and awesome moment, the darkness of the ages was dispelled – first Turkish domination, then Italian oppression and finally the era of the reactionary reign, the reign of bribery and personal favors, the reign of treachery and transgression …

The Erratic Leader

Once having consolidated power, Qaddafi embarked on a number of domestic and foreign policy initiatives, in which he showed himself to be as Nasser aide Gahazzen Bashir described him: 'dynamic in an irritating way, like a little boy, very erratic'.[43] Mohamed Heikal had observed, 'Like a *bedu,* Ghadaffi could change in a moment from one position to a completely opposite one.'[44] When I was in Khartoum in the 1990s, I asked a Sudanese friend who was at the time a high level government official, what he could tell me about Qaddafi. His answer was that the man was extremely erratic, and could be rational and pleasant at one moment, then fly into a rage the next. He could also shift alliances just as easily. Events were to prove he was on the mark.

This trait, commonly found in narcissistic personalities, was manifest in Qaddafi's foreign policy adventures, above all in his alliance policies. Early on, with the Nasserist dream of Arab unity in mind, he sought a confederation with Egypt and Syria. When Sadat, in 1972/73, had second thoughts, perceiving Qaddafi as a potential threat, the Libyan leader at first travelled to Cairo to iron out whatever problems there were, but then, on return to Libya, organized a 'people's march' on Egypt to push through the union. Egypt stopped the marchers at the border. Qaddafi issued assurances that their relations were sound, but an extremist Libyan group then tried to spark a coup against Sadat, and the situation deteriorated. By 1975, Qaddafi was actively propagandizing against Sadat and tensions soon degenerated into outright hostilities.

Pursuing his Nasserist dream of Arab unity, Qaddafi tried to launch union with Tunisia, which Bourghiba rejected. Initially Qaddafi supported the Polisario Front against Morocco, then abandoned it and made a union with Morocco. After his project for a Maghreb union failed, he turned to African states, proposing they join in a union which he would somehow re-baptize as 'Arab'. Qaddafi initially supported the Eritrean rebels but, as soon as Mengisthu assumed power, he shifted to a pro-Ethiopian stance.[45]

The Green Book

Hard to believe, but true: One of the unofficial titles attributed to Qaddafi in recent years is that of 'Leader and Thinker'. In fact, it is in this most unlikely realm that Qaddafi asserted his greatest and most bombastic claims to fame, which rest on the merits of his *opus magnus*, *The Green Book*. This work, which was published in Arabic in three parts between 1976 and 1979, has to be seen from three standpoints; first, its content: its fundamental theories and proposed applications; second, its function as the ideological foundation for the Qaddafi state order; and, third, its role as a means of quasi-deification/apotheosis of Qaddafi as a philosopher in the international community, or at least parts thereof.

The work itself can be read, digested and dispensed with in a relatively short period of time by any average reader, without any extraordinary intellectual, political or scientific knowledge. It is in sum a simple (if not simplistic), puerile attempt to conceptualize a social order in which true democracy reigns. Qaddafi argues against all forms of representative democracy in that they are 'representative' – i.e. not direct expressions of the people. His scheme for people's committees and a people's council represents an attempt to define a form of direct democracy, in his judgement, the definitive attainment of the same.

'The mere existence of a parliament means the absence of the people,' he writes. 'True democracy exists only through the direct participation of the people.'[46] Similarly, 'the party is a contemporary form of dictatorship, the modern instrument of dictatorial government. The party is the rule of a part over the whole.' Furthermore, 'The party system is the modern equivalent of the tribal or sectarian system. A society governed by one party is similar to one which is governed by one tribe or one sect.'

The solution lies in the creation of Popular Conferences, into which the people are divided. 'Each Basic Popular Conference chooses its secretariat. The secretariats of all Popular Conferences together form Non-Basic Popular Conferences. Subsequently, the masses of the Basic Popular Conferences select administrative People's Committees to replace government administration. All public institutions are run by People's Committees which will be accountable to the Basic Popular Conferences which dictate the policy and supervise the execution.'

As for law, Qaddafi wrote that natural law was based either on tradition or religion, so constitutions, which are not based on such natural sources, have no legitimacy. On press freedoms, he wrote: 'An individual has the right to express himself or herself even if he or she behaves irrationally to demonstrate his or her insanity.'

In the second part of *The Green Book*, Qaddafi addressed economic theory and practice. Here he stated that the wage system was essentially a slave system that must be abolished and replaced with a 'natural socialism'.

In his third and final part, Qaddafi dealt with social organization, from the family to the tribe, and nation. 'A tribe is an enlarged family,' he wrote. 'Similarly a nation is a tribe which has grown through procreation. The nation, then, is an enlarged tribe. The world is a nation which has been diversified into various nations. The world, then, is an enlarged nation … The essence of humanity is that of nation, the essence of nation is that of tribe, and the essence of the tribe is family.'

The tribe provides a 'behaviour pattern' for its members, as well as 'social protection' in the form of 'fines, revenge and defence'. 'Blood is the prime factor in the formation of the tribe.' From here, Qaddafi moved to the concept of the nation. 'The nation is … a social structure whose bond is nationalism; the tribe is a social structure whose bond is tribalism; the family is a social structure whose bond is humanity. These facts are self-evident.'

Qaddafi also dwelled on the difference between the sexes. His basic notion was that the two genders are different, biologically determined, and that the woman should essentially devote her time and energies to raising children. When children reach school age, they should have access to schools. Qaddafi stated categorically that 'State-controlled education ... is a method of suppressing freedom ... To force a human being to learn according to a set curriculum is a dictatorial act. To impose certain subjects upon people is also a dictatorial act.' He went on to state that: 'All methods prevailing in the world should be destroyed through a universal cultural revolution that frees the human mind from curricula of fanaticism which dictate a process of deliberate distortion of man's tastes, conceptual ability and mentality.' This doesn't mean all schools should be closed, but that people should be allowed to learn what they want. 'Ignorance will come to an end when everything is presented as it actually is and when knowledge about everything is available to each person in the manner that suits him or her.'

Regarding communication among all peoples, Qaddafi lamented the lack of a single human language but thought that 'it is only a matter of time before mankind achieves that goal, unless civilization should relapse'.

One can argue the merits or demerits of the concept presented in *The Green Book*, but when one compares it to the actual form of government that Qaddafi erected after the 1969 coup, one must conclude that his theory and his practice are on opposite sides of the universe. For all the rhetoric about people's power and direct democracy, the fact is that Qaddafi set up a dictatorial system soon after taking power, and that all power in fact lay in the hands of the man without any official positions – Qaddafi.

Shortly after his successful coup, Qaddafi banned all political parties, established top-down control over the press and wiped out trade unions.[47] The turning point to dictatorship came in 1973 with the Zwara declaration of 15 April – a proclamation calling for a new order which he deemed necessary in the light of the failure of Arab solidarity. The declaration eliminated all existing laws, banned opposition groups identified as 'political illnesses' – i.e. the Ba'athists, Communists, Muslim Brotherhood and so on – and called for arming the population, introducing an 'administrative revolution' and launching a cultural revolution to control the universities.[48] It was on this occasion that Qaddafi called for the institution of 'popular committees' as conceptualized in *The Green Book*. Some days later he expounded on his Third Universal Theory, which was the foundation for the Zwara declaration. This Third Universal Theory (i.e. neither communism nor capitalism, but a third way) was what *The Green Book* laid out. Qaddafi did not present it as a proposal, an idea or a concept but as *the Truth*. 'When we speak about the Third Universal Theory,' he told a group on 14 May, 'we stress that it is not made by man nor is it a philosophy, but it is based on truth.'

This is the crux of the matter. Although even Qaddafi had not had the chutzpah to assert this in so many terms, he apparently considered *The Green Book* as essentially a successor text to the Qur'an, in that it contains the Truth relating to man and society. Its claim to absolute truth is explicit: '*The Green Book* does not seek only to solve material problems,' he told Edmond Jouve. 'It also aims to open the way towards a global solution for the problems of society, in order to ensure the material and moral liberation of the individual, as well as his happiness. The aim of the Third Universal Theory is to guide him in this path by offering a theory of the liberation of needs in order to bring about the liberation of man.'[49]

The Green Book functioned as the text for the attempted brainwashing of the Libyan population. It was required reading in all schools at all levels; sculptures of *The Green Book* had been exhibited in public places, translations appeared in numerous languages and any visitor to Qaddafi's Libya would receive a copy as a matter of course.

Qaddafi's little book would have remained a tool for internal propaganda purposes had it not been for the fact that the regime, with the active participation of intellectual circles in the West who found *The Green Book* useful for a myriad of reasons, transformed it into a *bona fide* subject for academic discussion, with university theses on it accepted for graduate degrees. Most importantly, there have been a series of international conferences, seminars and so forth on the subject, which sought to establish Qaddafi and his *Green Book* as intellectual interlocutors.

The international symposia dedicated to the 'Thought of Muammar Qaddafi' portrayed him as if he were in the same intellectual or philosophical league as Edward Said. Qaddafi addressed one symposium in Benghazi in October 1979, and another followed in Madrid in December 1980. Speaking via satellite, the Libyan leader sent the following message:

The Orient has always been the cradle of civilization and of ideas which have changed the face of the world. We must not discount the possibility that it will once again give birth to a new world order. Mathematics, astronomy, medicine ... have been gifts to the world, invented by the Orient, Arabs and Muslims. In the same way, the Third Universal Theory, which has sprung from the Orient, could lead to the emergence of a new form of civilization, not reserved exclusively for the Orient, Arabs and Muslims. We would like the whole of humanity to benefit from it, just as it has been able to take advantage of the benefits of former civilizations.[50]

In April 1983, Benghazi played host to an 'International Symposium on the Thought of Muammar Qaddafi', which gathered about 1,000 'revolutionaries', including representatives of ten American organizations, among them African-Americans, Native Americans, Nation of Islam and others.[51] In addition to the symposia and seminars, published works on the thought of Qaddafi began to appear as a result of university studies oriented in this direction.[52] In many cases, such studies were also 'encouraged' by Libya financially.

All this is relevant to an understanding of Qaddafi's need for self-aggrandizement. As head of state he allocated funds and logistical resources for a number of such symposia and conferences, whose main function was to glorify the 'thought' of Muammar Qaddafi. *The Green Book* was the symbol of Qaddafi's overblown ego, his narcissistic claim to be the only one to embody the ultimate Truth. It is only fitting that the Libyan youth who launched the 2011 revolution seized on public images of *The Green Book* erected as monumental statues and smashed them to pieces.

Qaddafi: Thinker, Poet, Literary Genius

If *The Green Book* represented Qaddafi's claim to universal fame as an original political thinker whose social-political concept would solve all the problems of the world, other works presented his more literary-philosophical reflections on fundamental existential questions, what the Germans call 'God and the world'.

These volumes, though translated into other languages and issued in rather sumptuously bound editions, have not (yet) overwhelmed the literati or provoked cultural revolutions in other intellectual circles. One work, entitled *Escape to Hell and Other Stories*, which appeared in English in 1998, is a collection of Qaddafi's novels and essays. Presented with an introduction by no less a political intellectual than Pierre Salinger, the book is a collection of some of Qaddafi's fictional writings, which expand on and elaborate ideas that he had presented in a dry, more abstract form in his *Green Book*. The main thesis of the book is that everything urban is bad and everything rural (especially in the society of the desert nomads) is good. The juxtaposition is expressed in extreme terms, as befits a narcissistic personality, which can apprehend reality only in such black and white terms.

Thus, in 'The City', the first tale, we are told it is 'a nightmare ... a scavenging multitude' where '[o]ne engages in greed, toil, and is beset by want ... it is employment which forces one to live in a city'. This city is 'a graveyard of social connections and relations'. The anonymity of the city is striking: no one knows anyone, even the neighbours. 'Life in the city is merely a worm-like, biological existence where man lives and dies meaninglessly ... with no clear vision or insight. In either case, he is inside a tomb, whether he is living or dying.'

For Qaddafi, the greatest sin of the city is that it has swallowed up and destroyed what was once agricultural land. 'The city is anti-agriculture; it is built on arable land, and trees are uprooted for its construction. It tempts peasants to leave the land and become lazy beggars on its sidewalks. At the same time, the city devours agricultural production and demands more and more of it, although this agricultural production requires land and peasants. The city is anti-production ...' Above all, the city 'kills human and social feelings' and citizens have no compassion for their fellow man.

On the other hand, as depicted in 'The Village', the countryside is paradise on earth. 'Natural growth and living in the sunlight are encouraged, if not glorified. You do as the birds and flowers do, flying and opening up to the world ... People in the village and countryside will always remain linked by social bonds, connected in all moral and material matters.'

'Oh wise, kind-hearted people ... humanitarians: have mercy on children, and do not deceive them by making them live in the city.' Everything in the countryside is peaceful, clean, friendly, everybody knows everybody, there is no crime. 'There, life is social, and human; families and tribes are close. There is stability and belief. Everyone loves one another, and everyone lives on his own farm, or has livestock, or works in the village's service sector.'[53]

Among the other short stories in this volume is one entitled 'The Suicide of the Astronaut'. It tells of an astronaut who, having been in space, returned to earth and looked for some normal form of employment, but found none. He then met a peasant and asked for work on the farm. When the peasant asked him if he knew anything about tilling the earth, the astronaut responded with facts and figures gained from his experience as a space traveller, but the peasant was bored. The astronaut ended up committing suicide.

Another piece, entitled 'Death', begins with the question: 'Is death male or female?' Reflecting back on the heroic struggle of his forefathers, Qaddafi answered that death is male 'and is always on the offensive'. One fights against death, which is 'definitely male in all but these final situations, in which it turns out to be female'. Why has death become female? Because one has surrendered to her in the end.

Just how important his literary achievements, outside *The Green Book*, were to Qaddafi himself is hard to determine. When asked what he thought his legacy should be, he answered: 'In history books it should be written that I have liberated my people and, beyond that, decisively changed the world. I created Libya, I can also destroy it.' On another occasion, he had summed up his life's achievements, saying, 'I created a real utopia.'[54]

NOTES

—

1 Blundy, David and Andrew Lycett, *Qaddafi and the Libyan Revolution*, Little, Brown and Company, Boston, Toronto, 1987, p. 18.
2 Heikal, Mohamed, *The Road to Ramadan*, op. cit. p. 186.
3 Sicker, Martin, *The Making of A Pariah State: The Adventurist Politics of Muammar Qaddafi*, Praeger, New York, Westport, Connecticut, London, 1987, p. 56.
4 Ibid., p. 110.
5 Blundy, op. cit., p. 70.
6 Ibid., p. 180.
7 *Der Spiegel*, 'Reise in Gaddafis Hirn', 14/2011, 4 April 2011, pp. 90–91.
8 *Intifada Palestine*, 23 February 2011.
9 Mattes, Hanspeter, *Qaddafi und die islamische Opposition in Libyan*, Deutsches Orient-Institut, Hamburg, 1995, pp. 17, 127.
10 Blundy, op. cit., p. 30.
11 *Frankfurter Allgemeine Zeitung*, 28 February 2011.
12 Blundy, op. cit., pp. 9, 24.
13 Ibid., p. 24.
14 Ibid., p. 48.
15 *Intifada Palestine*, 28 February 2011.
16 *FAZ*, 27 February 2011. On foreign visits Qaddafi also took every opportunity to promote his grandiose self. When he visited Tunisia, he distributed 'on a grand scale, and in the style of purest kitsch: diamonds and above all glamorous clinking pendants, decorated with photos of himself …' Beau, Nicolas and Catherine Graciet, *La Régente de Carthage: Main basse sur la Tunisie*, La Découverte, Paris, 2009, p. 114.
17 Blundy, op. cit., pp. 22–23.
18 Mattes, op. cit., pp. 138–139.
19 Ibid., pp. 141–142.
20 *FAZ*, 15 March 2011.
21 Blundy, op. cit., pp. 150–151.
22 Heikal, op. cit., pp. 192–193.
23 Blundy, op. cit., pp. 146–148.
24 Sicker, op. cit., p. 60.
25 Heikal, op. cit., pp. 76–77.
26 Sicker, pp. 61, 65.
27 *FAZ*, 5 March 2011. The figures given were in the European currency: €145,000 and €500,000 respectively, *The Washington Post*, 15 March 2011.
28 Ibid., 11 March 2011.
29 Ibid., 19 March 2011.
30 There is some confusion as to Qaddafi's date of birth. Although he officially gives the date 1942, Blundy mentions that when he wanted to enter school in Misratah, and was over the age limit at 19, he procured a false birth certificate. It may be that this false document gave his birth date as 1942, so he may have been older than one at the time of the war experience, though still a baby.

31 Gaddafi, Muammar with Edmond Jouve, *My Vision: Conversations and Frank Exchanges of Views with Edmond Jouve*, translation into English by Angela Parfitt, John Blake, London, 2005, pp. 9–10, Blundy, op. cit., pp. 33–35.

32 Jouve, ibid., pp. 81–82, emphasis added. One can easily imagine what psychological terror the NATO bombing attacks provoked in the Libyan leader.

33 Bianco, Mirella, *Gadafi, Voice from the Desert*, translation by Margaret Lyle (Paris, Editions Stock, 1975), p. 4, paraphrased by Ayoub, Mahmoud Mustafa, *Islam and the Third Universal Theory: The Religious Thought of Ma'ammar al-Qadhdhafi*, KPI, London, 1987, p. 12.

34 Ibid., pp. 15, 13.

35 Blundy, op. cit., p. 36.

36 Ibid., p. 18.

37 Jouve, op. cit., p. 82.

38 Blundy, pp. 42, 46.

39 Ibid., pp. 47–50.

40 Fasanella, Giovanni, 'Gheddafi: Una Storia Italiana', *Cadoinpiedi*, 22 February 2011.

41 Blundy, op. cit., pp. 53–55.

42 Massimiliano Cricco and Federico Cresti, 'Psicogeopolitica di Gheddafi', I Quaderni Speciali di Limes – *Rivista italiana di Geopolitica*, 'La Guerra di Libia', April 2011, Anno 3. no. 2, Gruppo Editoriale L'Espresso, Roma. The US source referred to is the National Archives & Records Administration (NARA), Washington, DC, RG 59, SNF 1967–1969, POL 23–9 LIBYA, Research Memor.: 'Libya: Who Are Its Leaders?' From George C. Denney Jr, Director of Intelligence and Research of DOS to the Secretary of State. Appendix, Part I. Washington, DC, 10/9/69, secret.

43 Blundy, op. cit., p. 70.

44 Heikal, op. cit., p. 187.

45 Sicker, op. cit., pp. 69–89, Heikal, pp. 148–198.

46 *The Green Book*, Part One. All quotes are taken from the edition available at http://www.mathaba.net/gci/theory/gb1.htm.

47 Blundy, op. cit., p. 63.

48 Ibid., pp. 85–86.

49 Jouve, op. cit., pp. 37–38.

50 Ibid., pp. 35–36.

51 Sicker, op. cit., p. 120.

52 See Lohmann, Heiner, *Strukturen mythischen Denkens im Grünen Buch Mu'ammar al-Qaddafis: Eine kommunikationstheoretische Untersuchung zur Rationalität eines soziozentrischen Weltbildes im Islam mit einer Neuübersetzung des Grünen Buches im Anhang*, LIT Verlag Dr W. Hopf, Berlin, 2009, and Ayoub, op. cit.

53 Qaddafi, Muammar, *Escape to Hell and Other Stories*, Stanké, New York, 1998, pp. 29–57.

54 Blundy, op. cit., p. 26.

3

Hosni Mubarak: A Modern Ramses

In response to the mass uprising against his regime in January 2011, Hosni Mubarak was most conspicuous by his absence. This is not a British understatement, but a clinical fact, known to professional psychiatrists as the 'play dead reflex': a person who undergoes a traumatic experience, an event which seems to threaten him with injury or death, will respond with fear and will withdraw. If the subject, as in this case, is a political leader, such an encounter with an event quite outside his normal experience – an event that threatens his continued political existence – will produce not only fear, but also a sense of helplessness or terror. In his response to this utterly unforeseeable event, which places excessive demands on his ability to process the experience, the individual may undergo a series of reactions. Acting out of fear, he will first attempt flight and fall into paralysis – the 'play dead reflex'. In a depressive reaction, the individual may retreat or be gripped by anger, after which he may experience a sense of exhaustion and resignation. A third possible reaction, characterized as hysterical, involves retreat to a distance combined with an attempt to justify his behaviour. The subject is overcome by rage and irritation, and displays forms of dissociation.[1]

In the case of Mubarak, the full panoply of these clinical reactions was present. His first reaction was to flee the menacing reality of Tahrir Square and escape to his seaside refuge in Sharm al Sheikh. There he remained, holed up and protected from public view. Only after *five days* of unprecedented demonstrations, during which police deployed tear gas, water cannon and then live ammunition, killing an estimated 100 and injuring over 1,000, did he manage to muster the psychological strength to address his people. A statement by the president was imminent, the press announced. But Mubarak kept them waiting for hours. Then, speaking on television just after midnight on 29 January, he attempted to justify his actions. He said he 'deeply regret[ted] the loss of innocent lives among the protesters and police forces'. Ignoring the evidence of televised footage that had been viewed worldwide over the Internet, he claimed that the government had followed his 'instructions' to allow the citizens free expression: 'The government stayed committed to those instructions and that was obvious in the way police forces dealt with our youth, in taking initiatives to protect them ... before those protests turned into riots ...' A day earlier, 20 members of the Muslim Brotherhood had been detained, after the interior ministry accused them of fomenting chaos.

Further on in his speech, Mubarak identified the causes of the unrest in Egyptians' demands for 'halting unemployment and enhancing living conditions, fighting poverty and standing firmly against corruption.' He utterly ignored the fact that the people were not asking for reforms *per se* but for his resignation. Undeterred, he pledged to 'continue political, economic and social reforms for the sake of a free and democratic Egyptian community'. At the same time he charged that behind the protests was 'a larger scheme aimed at shaking stability and an attack on legitimacy'. A hundred Egyptians had died thus far in the confrontation, but the only concrete measure he announced was his sacking the government.

Days passed, and, despite the government-ordered disruption in cell phone and Facebook communications, the demonstrations continued, their numbers surging. Already prior to Mubarak's first speech, former IAEA chief Mohamed ElBaradei had joined the protests.[2] On 31 January, an estimated one-quarter million were in Tahrir Square and the military issued its first official statement, saying, 'The armed forces will not resort to the use of force against our great people' in guaranteeing its freedom of expression. For Mubarak, formally speaking as Commander in Chief of those Armed Forces, this constituted a second traumatic event, a move that foreshadowed the military's decision to actively join the movement. A couple of days earlier, Mubarak had nominated his chief of intelligence Omar Suleiman to the post of vice president but still clung to his office. His reluctance to name a vice president over the years had rightly been interpreted as expressing his intention to be president for life.

One million protesters filled Tahrir Square on 1 February, when Mubarak spoke for the second time. Continuing to attempt to justify himself, the *rais* charged that the protests 'which began with noble youths and citizens who practise their rights to peaceful demonstrations and protests ... were quickly exploited by those who sought to spread chaos and violence'. He announced that he had entrusted his new vice president with conducting a dialogue, but that 'there are some political forces who have refused this call to dialogue'. Therefore, addressing his remarks now 'directly to the people, its Muslims and Christians', Mubarak embarked on a series of lies, all fashioned to justify his continuing refusal to face reality and step down.

'I have never, ever been seeking power,' he claimed, before launching into self-praise for his military achievements 'in war and peace.' Furthermore, 'I am a man of the armed forces and it is not in my nature to betray the trust or give up my responsibilities and duties.' He insisted: 'I did not intend to nominate myself for a new presidential term. I have spent enough years of my life in the service of Egypt and its people.' He added several references to make clear that he was *not* resigning: 'I am now absolutely determined to finish my work,' and 'I will work *in the remaining months of my term*', etc. (emphasis added).

Despite Mubarak's pledge to secure public order and investigate those responsible for chaos, the following day a band of his loyalists organized by members of Mubarak's ruling National Democratic Party (NDP), armed with knives and clubs, rode horses and camels wildly into Tahrir Square. Reuters reported at least 3 dead and 1,500 wounded. Speaking to ABC on 2 February, Mubarak categorically stated that the choice was between him and chaos. Violence continued and escalated as the demonstrations expanded. By 5 February, the United Nations had estimated that 300 had died. Despite the government's attempt to toss crumbs to the hungry crowd, announcing a 15 per cent raise in salaries and pensions, and despite Suleiman's generic promise of legislative and constitutional reforms, the public pressure for Mubarak to leave office only escalated, buttressed by the support of trade unions and striking workers.

Through all the turmoil, again, Mubarak displayed the 'play dead reflex', retreating, this time, for nine days! On 10 February, while unprecedented numbers of Egyptians filled the streets and squares of Cairo, Alexandria and Suez expecting to hear him announce his resignation, Mubarak appeared on television in a somewhat dissociated state and simply offered more of the same. Lauding his service 'in over 60 years during war and peace', he recounted to his country's younger generation that he had been as young as they when he 'learned the Egyptian military honour, allegiance and sacrifice'; he had 'spent a lifetime defending [Egypt's] soil and sovereignty'; he had 'lived the days of the (Suez) crossing, victory and liberation'. 'It was the happiest day of my life when I raised the flag of Egypt over Sinai,' he trumpeted. His repeated references to 'September' (when his mandate would expire) and to his initiatives to prepare the transition made clear he was not prepared to budge.

There are three statements in what was to be his last speech that are of particular interest from the psychological standpoint. The first was his insistent denial that 'the current moment is not to do with myself, it is not to do with Hosni Mubarak, but is to do with Egypt, its present and the future of its children'. Here he was attempting to extricate himself from the conflict, to deny his personal role in the crisis. Professional psychiatric opinion reads this as a symptom of hysteria, whereby the person attempts internally to pull out of any responsibility. The second was his plea: 'I never sought power or fake popularity. I trust that the overwhelming majority of the people know who Hosni Mubarak is.' Here, a professional psychiatrist would see further indication of a loss of touch with reality. The people, after all, had just mobilized one million strong to send him the message that they wanted to have nothing to do with him. The statement that followed constituted an admission that indeed his people might not love him after all: 'It pains me to see how some of my countrymen are treating me today,' he said. Clinical analysis would see here a pathetic, yet truthful, statement uttered by a man who is suffering precisely because he has finally realized that he is *not* loved.

After the shoes starting flying in Tahrir Square, hitting the image of the president projected onto a huge screen, it must have dawned on Mubarak that, indeed, the time had come for him to bid farewell to his people. Significantly, it was Suleiman and not the president himself who announced the resignation. Mubarak's ego had been so devastated by events that he could not face the TV cameras and say, *I am stepping down*, i.e. *I am finally acknowledging reality*. He had apparently reached the final stage described in accounts of the 'play dead reflex': exhaustion, resignation and apathy.[3]

What made Mubarak resign? As he himself intimated in his addresses, foreign pressure had come down on him. He swore in his last speech that what he never had done and never would do is '[listen] to foreign dictations, whatever may be the source or pretext'. However, it is well documented that, as the crisis erupted, the Chief of Staff of the Army Sami Hafiz Annan was in the United States for consultations, and Defence Minister Hussein Tantawi soon followed. In the course of the revolution, the US Administration sent an envoy to Cairo to suggest that

Mubarak relent. President Barack Obama himself spoke to Mubarak by phone, and Secretary of State Hillary Clinton and Vice President Joe Biden contacted their Egyptian counterparts. During the entire period, American officers at all levels and from all branches received instructions to reopen their Egyptian contacts, military personnel who had been trained or had studied in the US. Given not only the political but also the financial support Washington has assured Egypt over decades, it is understandable that pressure from that quarter could be effective.

On 1 February 2011, Tantawi had gone to Tahrir Square and talked with demonstrators, signalling military support. On 10 February, prior to Mubarak's address, a major general shouted out to those in the square that all their desires would be satisfied.[4]

Narcissism and Pharaohs

To characterize Mubarak's behaviour during the revolutionary process as a 'play dead reflex' and clinical denial is accurate, but it does not provide a complete diagnosis of his psychological problem, because he also displays many manifestations of the *narcissistic personality disorder*.

In a certain sense, one could say that Mubarak 'inherited' narcissism, not from his parents, but from his two predecessors – Gamal Nasser and Anwar Sadat. Unlike Qaddafi, Mubarak did not himself establish a dictatorial state but, as historians agree, was bequeathed the state form established by Nasser, along with its leading institutions.[5] Although the institutions underwent some modifications under Sadat, the basic structure remained and, upon his death by assassination in 1981, then-Vice President Mubarak took it over, along with its political legacy. Both Nasser and Sadat had forged personality cults around themselves as supreme leaders, and it is as if Mubarak, stepping into the position of president, grew into the role of the narcissistic leader. As mental health professionals will point out, however, he must have had the personality structure to be able to step into such a role.

The phenomenon has a long history in Egyptian culture, reaching back to ancient times, where the figure of the Pharaoh symbolized state power in his person. Sadat reportedly told Mohamed Heikal, 'Gamal [Nasser] and I are the two last great pharaohs of Egypt', but, as Heikal goes on: 'He gave President Jimmy Carter a rather different version of the same theory; it was a mistake, he said, to look on him simply as a successor to Nasser – his real predecessor was Ramses II.'[6] Egyptians have long since attributed the same title to Mubarak, and a recent book, *The Last Pharaoh: Mubarak and the Uncertain Future of Egypt in the Volatile Mid East*, has provided useful material substantiating the claim. Author Aladdin Elaasar notes that all three 20th-century Egyptian leaders were admirers of Pharaoh Ramses II in particular, and for good reason: according to legend, Ramses II lived to be 99, and was Egypt's ruler for 66 of those years! He commissioned a huge number of gigantic monuments, statues and temples, including Abu Simbel and the Ramesseum. One such statue of Ramses II was moved by Mubarak in 2006 from a central square to the museum.[7]

The regime that Nasser set up featured the role of the military as an integral part of the state, whose officers served in government posts, the diplomatic corps, the intelligence and security organizations and the media, which Nasser nationalized. He eliminated pre-existing political parties, and his Arab Socialist Union (later renamed the National Democratic Party by Sadat) established one-party rule. When hundreds of judges refused to join the party, Nasser fired them in an act that was to become known as the massacre of the judges.[8] Nasser's dictatorship, which Mubarak inherited, has been classified as a 'triple threat', that is, a dictatorship which combines the elements of three types: the personalist (where power is concentrated in one person), the military and the single-party dictatorship.[9]

The military maintained its leading role in social institutions and in the economy, but, since it was still a draft army, it could not be relied upon to serve the interests of the regime or its leader above those of the people. This was to prove to be Mubarak's Achilles' heel in the 2011 revolution.

But his internal security apparatus and intelligence apparatus, the rightly feared Mukhabarat, were under his direct control, and he deployed them mercilessly against any and all presumed or real enemies. The hated Mukhabarat, which was dissolved on 15 March 2011, was notorious for its brutal torture methods, comparable to those deployed by the State Security (Stasi) of Communist East Germany. Citizens were arrested on the slightest pretext, protected by the Emergency Law and subjected to violent interrogations punctuated by torture. I remember my late friend, Adel Hussein, the editor of an opposition newspaper *Al Shaab*, who had been tortured in an Egyptian jail. When he came to the US for a visit and was invited to dinner with friends of mine, the long-term after-effects of his traumatic experience surfaced. The friends had a dog, and although it was quite a friendly puppy, wagging its tail, Adel reacted to it as if it were a mortal threat. It turned out the Egyptian authorities had used dogs to torture him. The widespread torture under Mubarak has been documented by human rights groups and reported on inside the country by courageous journalists like Alaa Al Aswany.[10]

Mubarak upheld the tradition set by Nasser of one-party rule with his NDP. Although, formally speaking, other 'opposition' parties were allowed to exist, the election laws were so rigged as to prevent any one or combination of them to challenge the NDP's monopoly on power. Presidential elections did not come into being until 2005; instead, Mubarak had himself nominated as the sole candidate, and invited the population to 'elect' him in a referendum every six years. His percentages were always in the upper 90 per cent range.

Having consolidated the institutions of the Nasserite era under his presidential authority, Mubarak gradually adopted the external trappings due an absolute ruler. He made certain that his person and his public image would not be besmirched by adverse press opinion, by personally nominating the editors of the leading Egyptian dailies and maintaining government control over printing and distribution.[11] Clauses in the Penal Code and Press Law made it illegal to 'undermine the dignity of the head of state', and this was strictly enforced. Saad Eddin Ibrahim of the Ibn Khaldun Centre for Development Studies was indicted for defamation and sentenced to seven years. He had written about a trend in the Arab world towards inherited presidencies.[12] Another illustrious example is that of Ibrahim Eissa, whose crime it was to have reported on rumours about Mubarak's failing health – a taboo. He too was indicted but then pardoned. When such allusions to the president's illnesses surfaced in the international press, government newspaper editors received orders to stress his good health and to denounce contrary reports as part of a Zionist conspiracy. Later, when Eissa spoke out against the system as such and criticized the head of state directly, his newspaper *al-Dustur* was bought by one Sayed Badawi, owner of al-Hayat TV, and Eissa was fired.[13]

In keeping with the needs of the narcissist not only to stave off negative criticism but to exalt his person, Mubarak sought the accumulation of official positions and titles, honorary or real. He has had more than his share. He was Chairman of the NDP, Commander-in-Chief of the Armed Forces and Military Ruler, Chairman of the G-15, Chairman of the Arab Summit, Chairman of the Organization of African Unity, Secretary General of the Non-Aligned Movement, among others.[14] His wife, Suzanne, far outdid her husband in gathering titles, all related to her ostensibly humanitarian engagement in social programmes, and the list is impressive: 'She serve[d] as a patron of the children's television series, *Alam Simsim*, Egypt's version of *Sesame Street.*' She was the 'honorary president of Rotary Clubs of Egypt ... and ... Founder and Chairperson of the Egyptian Society for Childhood and Development, Initiator and Founder of Egyptian Children's Literature Centre for Documentation Research and Information, Founder of the National History Museum for Children, President of the Advisory Board to the National Council for Childhood and Motherhood, President of the Egyptian National Women Committee, President of the First and Second National Conference on Women, Initiator of the Universal Law on Children, President of the Egyptian Section of the International Board of Books for Young People, President of the Egyptian Red Crescent Society and the National Campaign for Safe Blood Transfusion, Vice President of COMEST, and President of the National Council of Women, to mention a few.' In reality, many of these honorary titles served as covers for profit-making activities that contributed to increasing the considerable financial holdings of Mubarak and his clan. It is estimated that Mrs Mubarak took in US$5 billion a year through such benevolent activities.[15]

Following his downfall, the authorities moved to erase commemorative references to the presidential couple in public places. As posted on the website of the Egyptian State Information Service (SIS) on 22 April, the Cairo Court for Urgent Matters that day handed down a decision whereby their names 'be removed from all public facilities, squares, streets and libraries'.

Just how much Hosni Mubarak, his wife Suzanne or their sons Alaa and Gamal were worth is an open question – at least until the post-Mubarak authorities can complete thorough investigations. Press reports cite reliable sources that estimate the magnitude of the Mubarak clan's wealth. ABC News calculated on 2 February, when Mubarak was still formally in power, that his family's assets were somewhere between US$40 billion and US$70 billion. Much of the money came from business partnerships with foreign entities, whereby the Egyptian partner is guaranteed 51 per cent. Add to this funds siphoned off from foreign aid programmes, grants, etc. perhaps not excluding the US$1.5 billion per year that Egypt receives from the US in 'aid'. The Mubaraks reportedly own real estate in New York, Los Angeles, London and along the Red Sea.[16] The Egyptian State Information Service referred to investigations confirming the massive wealth of the former First Family. New Justice Minister Abdel Aziz el-Gendy told *Al Ahram* that they possessed chalets, villas, palaces and apartments both in Egypt and abroad, and had multiple bank accounts. Together, the two held estates of US$25 billion.[17]

The announcement by US and European authorities that the Mubarak family accounts abroad would be frozen and seized was welcomed in Cairo, but the revolutionary forces also insisted that legal proceedings be brought against the former regime leaders. On 10 April, the public prosecutor 'requested and required' that Mubarak and his two sons present themselves for questioning, regarding responsibility in the killing of civilians (at that point in time estimated to have been 846) as well as illegal financial activities. Amazingly, Mubarak denied everything. In an audio message he had pre-recorded for broadcast on Al Arabiya that day, Mubarak stated that he felt 'a lot of pain' because of the 'unjust campaign' against him, a campaign full of 'lies, distortions and incitement', and that he would defend himself against the same. He pledged his full cooperation with the government and judicial authorities 'to ask any government in the world to expose my assets abroad since I took office'. He added: 'I want to make sure that the Egyptian people know I only own assets in a bank account inside this country.' Practising psychiatrists will confirm that this kind of behaviour is common among persons with a personality disorder who are caught in some criminal endeavour. They will seek to uphold their self-image as innocent as a means to stabilize themselves internally. As a result of his removal from office, Mubarak did undergo an internal breakdown, manifest also in signs of physical illness for which he was relocated to a clinic in Sharm al Sheik.

On the legal front, he was indicted in mid-May for misappropriating state funds and enriching himself illegally. Ten days later charges were brought against him and his sons for ordering the killing of protesters. As of 1 June, Mubarak was in such poor health that doctors declared him unable to leave his hospital bed. They said he had had a heart attack, and his lawyer, Farid el-Deeb, said he suffered from cancer as well. Nonetheless, the former president was brought to trial in Cairo on 3 August. In what must have been the ultimate humiliation, he was wheeled into the courtroom on a stretcher and then placed inside a cage, together with his two sons, Gamal and Alaa. The dramatic sequence, covered live on Egyptian state television, was a cathartic experience for the millions of Egyptians watching it, especially for those who had lost a relative during the revolution. Though satisfied that the dictator was finally being brought to justice, many expressed scepticism about his alleged illness. As one Egyptian quipped: 'He can't be that sick: he's still dyeing his hair.'

The charges brought against Mubarak were serious. He stood accused of abusing power, amassing wealth, rigging gas prices to Israel and – most serious – conspiring in the premeditated and attempted murder of protesters during the 18-day uprising, a charge also launched against former Interior Minister Habib el-Adly and six aides. Mubarak was convicted on 2 June 2012 and sentenced to life in prison. The court accused Mubarak's sons of illegally amassing wealth and abusing power. The accusation was that they had accepted five villas worth more than US$5 million.

True to form, Mubarak rejected the charges. 'I deny all these accusations completely,' he stated in court. Field Marshal Mohamed Hussein Tantawi, the head of the military council that took over after Mubarak's overthrow, testified in September in a closed session. Interrogated regarding Mubarak's role in the ruthless repression of demonstrators, he claimed he was not present at meetings during which such matters were decided. His testimony raised questions regarding the intentions of the military to pursue justice in the case of Mubarak, and to hand over power to a civilian government.

As for Suzanne Mubarak, she too reportedly suffered a heart attack. Detained on charges of illegal acquisition of wealth and indicted, she was released on 17 May 2011 after having relinquished her assets – a villa and multiple bank accounts worth about US$4 million– to the state. This bought her temporary freedom. In June she faced further corruption charges regarding misappropriation of public funds, channelling public works projects to family members and abusing positions in public office.

Childhood Trauma

Although Hosni Mubarak had no documented childhood traumas comparable to those of Muammar Qaddafi, he did suffer under a severe inferiority complex and his family was very, very poor.

He never spoke of his father's occupation, which he was ashamed of. His father worked as court concierge and earned less than 5 Egyptian pounds per month. Taking out his frustrations on his son, Mubarak senior was very tough on the boy, beating him with or without cause. He also made his son work in the fields beginning at the age of six, and pocketed whatever money Hosni made. The future president was apparently so ashamed of his humble beginnings, that he shunned contact with his extended family in Kafr-al-Meselha in the Nile Delta region where he was born. Quite contrary to traditional practice, he did not visit members of his extended family, and went back to his hometown only once, in 2005, when he was exploring the possibilities of organizing a referendum to prolong his mandate still further. Since his ouster, members of his extended family have aired these complaints openly on Egyptian TV; Hosni did not go back home for important family occurrences like weddings or funerals. He did not even visit the grave of his father, a fact that raises questions about how he dealt with his father's death psychologically.

At primary school at Kafr-al-Meselha, Mubarak's propensity to tell tall tales earned him the nickname of 'liar', and classmates also called him 'thief'. In secondary school he was known as 'Hosni Al Khabbassa', a troublemaker, who, through chronic lying, generated conflict among his friends and instigated misunderstandings. All these traits are typical of the young narcissist. There should be no wonder that Mubarak concealed all information about his childhood and that the CV which the Egyptian authorities drafted for him was never shared.

His wife, Suzanne, who is much higher up on the social ladder than he, reportedly forbade any visits back home, and declined to invite any of her husband's country bumpkin relatives to attend the wedding of their son Alaa. Suzanne Sabet is the daughter of an Egyptian doctor and a nurse from Wales; she frequented the best schools in Heliopolis, where she mastered English. After marrying Hosni, she continued her studies and obtained a graduate degree before entering the scene as First Lady. It was Jihan Sadat, her predecessor, who taught her the dos and don'ts of being a First Lady, and she was, reportedly, a good student.

Hosni Mubarak always felt ill at ease in the presence of persons of higher social rank, be they aristocrats or academics. Since he came from a poor family, he sought to compensate by making a career in the military. He succeeded in the effort, and used his military credentials to open doors to political power. But even in this phase of his career, his character was placed in question. While in the air force, he earned the reputation of a social climber. More serious was the charge that he was a traitor because he spied on his associates and informed his superiors of their activities. Some accounts say he was convicted of taking bribes while a military officer, though firm evidence is lacking.

The Making of a Narcissist

Mubarak inherited the institutions of a dictatorship and, instead of dismantling them, perpetuated them in his own image. This was a gradual process, a process through which he also consolidated a personality cult around his person that was befitting a Sadat or a Nasser, or a Ramses II. Several accounts say his leadership style was 'low-key' and 'businesslike'[18] at least during his first ten years in office. In fact, he avoided the press fanfare that Sadat and his wife had enjoyed, and even gave orders to the press not to cover any news of his wife or sons, nor to publish their photographs.[19] (Some construed this to mean that Mubarak thought Sadat's wife's high-profile public image had fed popular discontent with her husband's government.)[20]

This changed radically at the latest after 1990. It was at that point that Mubarak became totally self-centred and adamant about establishing his one-man, one-party rule. He began to place his personal security above all other considerations, defining that as the central responsibility of the army and the Republican Guard. Ordinary citizens had to reorganize their plans for travel through the city, for example, in consideration of the president's itinerary. If Mubarak had to move from his residence, which is on the road that leads to the airport, to somewhere in the city centre, all traffic in Cairo would be blocked for a radius of 20 kilometres to allow free passage for the seemingly endless presidential motorcade. And the affected motorways in Cairo remained closed to traffic for between two and three hours before his motorcade was to pass, for example, to the airport. If a woman in a taxi were in labour or a man with a heart attack were not able to reach hospital facilities due to roadblocks that was unfortunate but essentially irrelevant. This practice of paralysing Cairo traffic for the passage of the president, officially rationalized as an anti-terrorist precaution, was introduced long before the assassination attempt against Mubarak in 1995, which occurred on foreign soil.

The First Lady enjoyed a comparable level of high security wherever she went. I remember during a visit to Cairo, when I wanted to walk through the Old City, I was stopped by armed guards and held in place for an hour. There were soldiers every 100 metres and sharpshooters stationed on every roof, as if they expected a showdown with Islamist terrorists. It turned out Mubarak's wife, known popularly as Mamma Suzanna, was on her way to a ladies' association reception.

Mubarak's new leadership style was characterized by extreme arrogance, especially in his relations with the people he was supposed to represent and protect, the ordinary citizen. This is something one finds often in narcissistic personalities. In public speeches, he came across as being extremely distant. In part this resulted from his total dependence on reading from a written text. As was evident even in his last speeches during the revolution, he mouthed the words without giving any hint that there was conviction, let alone emotion, behind them. If, on occasion, he were to speak freely without any text or notes, he was wont to adopt a coarse, when not vulgar, language, which shocked his listeners. During one Labor Day speech, for example, he departed from his prepared text and lit into a tirade against his citizens, accusing them of being greedy and over-consuming. He was eager to blame the problems of Egypt on its people, charging, for example, that if the standard of living were low, that must be due to unchecked population growth. Egyptians should have fewer children was the message. This denotes the narcissistic lack of empathy, and his contempt for people he considers underlings.

Many political figures will deliver a speech from a written text and, more often than not, it is prepared by a speechwriter, not by the speaker. Indisputably, this was the case with Mubarak; following one speech he delivered at Cairo University, for instance, he gathered the pages together and handed them haughtily to his assistant, saying, 'This is your speech, take it.'

Those who know the former president personally have testified to the fact that he is, to put it charitably, not a deep thinker. They characterize him as being rather shallow and add that he has always had problems with reading; that is, he could read and write, but had difficulties in reading a text and grasping its content. He had problems in comprehending ideas, which was clear in his unwillingness to hold long discussions. This became manifest whenever one of his advisors briefed him on an urgent problem, expecting him to respond in an appropriate form. When his Minister of Irrigation Dr Muhamed Nasser El Din Allam reported to him on the discussions during a regional conference of irrigation ministers, where the complicated Nile problem was on the agenda, he gave him only ten minutes of his time and, thanking him for his work, said he thought the issue could be dealt with 'in the future'.

In such encounters he would tend to speak *ex cathedra*, barking out orders and judgements as if transmitted from a High Authority, and thus embodying the Truth. One Egyptian intellectual who had met Mubarak on a couple of occasions told me that he would start a conversation with his index finger raised and, pointing it menacingly at his interlocutor, would say, do this or do that. Lacking any of the charisma that Nasser had, Mubarak would rely on the projection of the authority of his office. In the eyes of his people, such behaviour made him a ridiculous figure, a laughing stock. The most popular nickname for him was 'the laughing cow', inspired by his resemblance to a French dairy product, known as '*La vache qui rit*'.

His need to protect his superior self-image explains his policy in appointing of public officials: anyone perceived to be qualified, dignified and self-respecting would be ignored and sycophants would get the jobs. Thus, 'ministers fall over each other to extol the president, laud his wisdom, and sing the praises of his amazing and historic decisions'.[21]

Mubarak was also famous for his stubbornness and contrariness. Some political analysts in Egypt attribute his refusal to re-establish diplomatic relations with Iran to this obstinacy. He was known also to do the opposite of what the press recommended out of sheer mule-headedness. Thus, if journalists wanted to have a public figure dumped, they would heap praise on him, knowing that Mubarak's profile would lead him to stymie the wishes of the press. Journalists loyal to the president would act in a contrary manner, damning anyone Mubarak disliked. One notorious case was that of ElBaradei. For as long as he had earned honours at home and abroad, he was praised. But 'as soon as

Egyptians spoke out and called on ElBaradei to stand for the presidency, the scribes … switched to the opposite extreme'.[22]

Collective Traumas

If Mubarak was spared any major traumas as a child, he certainly had his share as an adult. These were collective, not personal, traumas but they left an indelible imprint on his narcissistic personality. The first major shock came in 1967, with the humiliating defeat during the six-day war against Israel. The entire Arab world was thunderstruck, but especially Egypt, the unquestioned leader of the Arab world under its charismatic leader Nasser. Nasser tendered his resignation and it was only massive popular demand that kept him in power. As part of Nasser's reorganization after the defeat, Mubarak became director of the Air Academy and two years later was promoted to Chief of Staff of the Air Force.

The 1967 war represented a trauma which became incorporated into the saga of Arab suffering under Israeli might, roughly comparable to the trauma of the Serbs' defeat in 1389. The October War of 1973 provided the collective compensatory response, which would not long after be eternalized in popular mythology. The 1973 war, through which Egypt regained the Sinai, was a boon to Sadat politically, and for Mubarak it presented the stuff out of which a grand tapestry of heroism could be woven. To be sure, as commander of the Air Force, Mubarak performed well, for which he was promoted in 1974 to Air Marshal of the Egyptian Air Force.

But, if one reads the Gospel according to Mubarak on that 1973 conflict, one learns that it was the first air strike delivered on 6 October that decided the outcome of the war. The soldiers, artillery, tank units, logistics, etc. were merely secondary props, so to speak, on the stage. Mubarak's yes-men hailed him as the 'champion of the air strike', and this provided him with the credentials to maintain presidential rule through farcical referenda every six years. One minister of information went on national television to announce that Mubarak's heroic performance in the 1973 war was more than sufficient to allow him the presidency for life. And every year, on the 25 April anniversary of the Sinai liberation, Mubarak would wax eloquent. In 2006, for example, he spoke of 'an immortal day of Egypt's history and a glorious day for Egypt's people and the Armed Forces', a day on which 'the sad leaf of the 1967 defeat with its bitterness and suffering was turned over and with the restoration of this dear spot of Egypt's territory, the country's dignity and its compatriots' pride were redeemed as well'. As noted above, he tried to manipulate the masses during the revolution by recalling his 1973 exploits.

Since Mubarak's ouster, the myth of his central heroic role has been openly contested. Mohamed Heikal, an aide to Nasser and insider in the subsequent regimes, stated on 19 February 2011 on television that the function of the Air Force in 1973 had been largely psychological, i.e. to provide cover to the ground troops. Furthermore, the daughter of former Chief of Staff Eldin Elshazli (who passed away on 10 February, the day Mubarak resigned) publicly accused Mubarak of having lied about the war in function of his own self-aggrandizement. As reported in *Almasry al Youm* on 26 February 2011, her charge was that Mubarak had even doctored photos and other documents to enhance his role in the 1973 war, as opposed to her father's role. She said that she intended to take legal action.[23] Such lying in the interests of self-aggrandizement is often displayed by narcissistic personalities.

Not many years after the 1973 war which rehabilitated Egypt's image, Anwar Sadat was to embark on a journey with no return: his historic visit to Jerusalem and speech to the Knesset calling for peace, followed by the Camp David Accords signed on 17 September 1978 in Washington with Israeli Prime Minister Menahim Begin in the presence of President Jimmy Carter. That act, which led to signing a peace treaty with Israel, earned Egypt an expulsion from the Arab League and put Sadat on a target list for elimination. His assassination in 1981 constituted a further traumatic event, which Mubarak experienced first-hand. Although no open discussion of the matter was thinkable under the Mubarak regime, since its demise on 10 February Egyptian press accounts have raised the hypothesis that Mubarak may in fact have been involved in, or privy to, plans for killing Sadat. Whether this is true or not, the fact is that Mubarak exploited Sadat's assassination as the pretext to reinstate the hated Emergency Law which the demonstrators in Tahrir Square demanded be abrogated.

Camp David also earned Egypt a steady flow of US financial aid, to the tune of US$1.5–2 billion per year. Mubarak's agreement to join the US–UK-led war on Iraq in 1991 may very well have been conditioned by the fact that the US, Europe and the Gulf states promised to reward him by forgiving a whopping US$20 billion in debt as a thank-you for the support. As a result he was considered, like Sadat before him, as a lackey of US interests. His behaviour vis-à-vis the Palestinians after 2000 would only confirm this view. Not only did he uphold the embargo of Gaza following the 2006 elections that brought Hamas to power, but he initiated the underground wall intended to block tunnels into Gaza. In late 2008, during a visit by then-Israeli Foreign Minister Tzipi Livni, he was informed of Israeli plans for a war against Gaza. Documents leaked by WikiLeaks later confirmed that he had not only acquiesced to the attack but had solicited it.

Yet, Mubarak had perpetuated the myth of his Egypt as the stalwart ally of the Palestinians in their quest for an independent state and peace. The last myth he propagated was that he would be president for life, and that that life perhaps might never end. One popular joke circulating at his expense goes as follows ...

Some years ago, US President Bill Clinton, Russian President Vladimir Putin and Egyptian President Mubarak were summoned by God, who imparted to them the message that the world would end within two days. Clinton went on national television to announce that he had both good and bad tidings. First, the good news, that God does exist, and then the bad news, that the world would end within days. Putin addressed his citizenry saying he had two negative reports to deliver: first, that God existed, which meant that the entire edifice of Marxist–Leninist ideology was undermined, and then, that the world would soon end. Mubarak spoke to his people in an upbeat tone, reporting on two positive developments: first, that he had just concluded a successful meeting with God, and second, that he had been assured that he would remain Egypt's leader until the end of time.

NOTES

—

1 Längle, Alfried, 'Personality Disorders and Genesis of Trauma: Existential Analysis of Traumatized Personality Disorders', in *Existenzanalyse* 22, 2, 4–18, 2005, pp. 1–24. The 'play dead reflex' in relation to Post-Traumatic Stress Disorder (PTSD), pp. 6–7.

2 When ElBaradei returned to Egypt a year earlier, he received a hero's welcome, with thousands going to the airport and flaunting security warnings to greet him. The authorities, eager to play down his popularity, but fearing international press exposure if they blocked the crowds, decided instead to escort ElBaradei out of the airport through a gate where his supporters could not reach him. Alaa Al Aswany, op. cit., pp. 135–137.

3 Längle, op. cit., p. 6.

4 Frank Nordhausen, "Ägypten: Die Sieger des Tahrir-Platzes', in Frank Nordhausen, Thomas Schmid (Hg.), *Die Arabische Revolution: Demokratischer Aufbruch von Tunesien bis zum Golf*, Ch. Links Verlag, Berlin, October 2011, pp. 47, 55–57.

5 See, for example, Tripp, Charles and Roger Owen, eds., *Egypt under Mubarak*, Routledge, London and New York, 1989.

6 Heikal, Mohamed, *Autumn of Fury: The Assassination of Sadat*, Andre Deutsch Limited, London, 1983, p. 74.

7 Elaasar, Aladdin, *The Last Pharaoh: Mubarak and the Uncertain Future of Egypt in the Volatile Mid East*, Beacon Press, Montana, 2009, p. 48, 51.

8 Ibid., pp. 22–23.

9 Ezrow, Natasha M. and Erica Frantz, *Dictators and Dictatorships: Understanding Authoritarian Regimes and their Leaders*, The Continuum International Publishing Group, New York, 2011, pp. 20–23, 270–273.

10 Op. cit., pp. 159–180.

11 Elaasar, op. cit., pp. 183–184.

12 Ibid., pp. 171–172.

13 Al Aswany, op. cit., pp. 59, 58, 190–191.

14 Elaasar, op. cit., p. 304.

15 Ibid., p. 306.

16 ABC News, Feb. 2, 2011, guardian.co.uk, Feb. 4.

17 Ben Jelloun, Tahar, *Arabischer Frühling: Vom Wiedererlangen der arabischen Würde*, translation from the French by Christiane Kayser, Bloomsbury Verlag GmbH, Berlin, 2011, p. 59.

18 Tripp and Owen, op. cit. This was in 1989.

19 Darraj, Susan Muaddi, *Hosni Mubarak*, Chelsea House, New York, 2007, p. 60.

20 Amin, Galal, op. cit., pp. 113–114. Amin also details the means through which the Mubarak regime maintained top-down control over the press, by hiring and firing editors, p. 115.

21 Al Aswany, op. cit., pp. 14, 26. Al Aswany drives home the point about deliberate hiring of sycophants and incompetents, by detailing that the prime minister was someone who had never been in politics, a social solidarity minister had been in the postal authority, etc., p. 26.

22 Ibid., pp. 15–16. Al Aswany displays a keen understanding of the self-image of leaders like Mubarak. 'History teaches us that all autocratic rulers consider

themselves great heroes and live in such a state of perpetual self-delusion that they are able to justify all their misconduct and even the crimes they perpetrate. This ... is known as "dictator's solitude". The dictator lives in complete isolation from the lives of his compatriots and does not know what is really happening in his country. After he has been in power for years, a group of friends and rich relatives forms around him and their extravagant lifestyle keeps them apart from the way of life of ordinary people, and so the dictator loses any awareness of the poor and has absolutely no contact with real life. An image of it is conveyed to him in reports by various security agencies, but these agencies always think it is in their interests to put a gloss on the bleak reality to avoid angering the dictator. They often compete with each other ... Sometimes they make up imaginary conspiracies ... [The ministers'] only concern is to retain the approval of the ruler who appointed them and who can dismiss them at any moment. They never confront the ruler with the truth, but always tell him what he would like to hear', p. 36.

23 http://www.almasry-alyoum.com/article2.aspx?ArticleID=288933&IssueID=2058, quoted in http://en.wikipedia.org/wiki/Hosni_Mubarak

4

Zine El-Abidine Ben Ali: All in the Family

Sometimes *vox populi* – the voice of the people – can be a valuable guide to interpreting historical events. Amor Ben Hamida, who was in Tunisia at the time of the '2011 revolution' and wrote a short book on his experience, reported on a discussion he had with his taxi driver not long after Zine El-Abidine Ben Ali had delivered his final speech and fled the country. 'To be honest,' the cabby said, 'Ben Ali was not all that bad as people now say. His entourage, in particular, his wife, bewitched him. They were a bad influence.' He went on to note that those who celebrated his downfall had cheered him when he made his 1987 coup, marvelled at his bloodless takeover and upholding the constitution. 'I tell you,' he said, 'the man is the victim of his entourage … He listened to that viper of a woman for too long!'[1]

Whatever the actual dynamic in their relationship was at the beginning, there can be no doubt that in the Tunisian case the leading narcissist was not the man sitting on the president's throne but the lovely First Lady in her boudoir. Any insightful observer who has seen photographs of the woman or watched any of her many television appearances would suspect that the attractive woman with the haughty demeanour might have an overblown image of herself. She might be a narcissist. Just as Qaddafi's 'umbrella trick' was a psychologically tell-tale moment, Leila's visit to the Tunisian Central Bank to pick up her pocket money for the move into exile was a clear hint that the woman might be diagnosed as someone with a severe narcissistic personality disorder.

The story, which first appeared in the Algerian *DNA* on 14 January and was picked up by French television and press, is that Leila waltzed into the Central Bank of Tunisia one day and demanded 1.5 tons of gold bullion, worth US$5 billion. According to the 17 January edition of *Le Monde*, the information (which French intelligence had) came from a Tunisian source close to the Central Bank. When the bank's governor refused to deliver without a written order, Leila went to her husband who, after initially balking, acquiesced.

The director general of the Bank officially denied the story. One explanation for the discrepancy in the accounts suggested by French intelligence is that the First Lady had actually made the transaction back in December 2010, not January, and taken the gold out of the country at that time, depositing it in Switzerland. *DNA* broke the story on the day of their escape from Tunisia to Saudi Arabia, where they settled in at the former palace of King Fahd.[2] After Ben Ali's removal, Abdelfattah Amor, president of a new commission investigating corruption, revealed what its members had discovered behind a movable wall of bookshelves in the president's private residence in Sidi Bou Said, a coastal city north of Tunis: dubbed the 'treasure of Ali Baba', it included stacks of cash (dollars, euros and Tunisian dinars), and caskets filled with diamonds, pearls and other jewels, estimated to be worth US$28 million. They had, however, made off with a fortune. They had smuggled vast amounts out of the country and put it in safe keeping in foreign banks. *Forbes* magazine estimated in 2007 that Ben Ali was worth US$5 billion and Leila, US$4 billion. After the Swiss government issued a ban on all family members selling any real estate, it appeared that the safe keeping abroad was not so safe after all.[3]

Leila Ben Ali Trabelsi, now publicly damned as the most hated woman in Tunisia and dubbed 'the Regent' in a book on the regime, bears general biographical traits of a narcissist: she was born in 1957 into a very poor family, with 11 siblings. Her father had a boutique, which sold items that young men gave their fiancées such as dried fruits, henna, sweets and nuts. Her father died in 1970, and her poor mother had to work for some time in a public bath (hammam). The censorship that prevailed under Ben Ali made it impossible for details of her childhood to appear in print, and the only ascertained fact about her which the press was allowed to print was that she became a hairdresser. This account, however, may not be true. It turns out that Leila had a good friend, the owner of a hair salon, who was also called Leila Trabelsi: hence the confusion. *Vox populi*, in the person of the Tunisian taxi driver, reported the story that she had been involved in some drug affair, from which Ben Ali extricated her.[4]

The published facts about her relationship to Ben Ali fill in the picture of a clinical case of narcissism, *à deux*. They met in the 1980s at a time when Ben Ali, who had studied at military and intelligence institutions in France and the United States, was fully integrated into the military/intelligence apparatus. He had served as General Director of National Security from 1977–1980, Secretary of State for National

Defence (1984) and was to move on to become Interior Minister (1986) and Prime Minister (1987). Ben Ali had been dispatched to Poland as ambassador in 1980, and returned in 1984. Although the exact dates of their meeting are not clear, it must have been some time before 1986 when their first child, Nesrine, was born out of wedlock. At the time Ben Ali was married to Na'ima el-Kafy, the daughter of General Mohammad el-Kafy, who had sponsored Ben Ali's career and was the mother of his three girls. Ben Ali maintained Leila as his concubine in a nearby villa and, after becoming president through a coup in November 1987, left his wife. He married Leila in 1992 and a second daughter, Halima, was born that year. Their first son was born in 2005 and, as their choice of name indicated – Mohammed Zine El-Abidine Ben Ali – they destined him to become the dynastic successor to his father. *Vox populi* dubbed him 'the crown prince'.[5]

The relationship between Ben Ali and Leila conforms to what the clinical literature describes in cases where beauty and fame play a role in the choice of partner. 'When the narcissistic personality falls in love,' Kernberg writes, 'the idealization of the loved object may center on physical beauty as a source of admiration' – as in the case of Leila – 'or on power, wealth or fame as attributes' – as with Ben Ali – 'to be admired and unconsciously incorporated as parts of the self.'[6]

Yet, as mentioned, it was not an acceptable encounter between two narcissists; after all, one of them was already married. When such a relationship develops, psychoanalysts speak in terms of 'reverse triangulation.' In this textbook example, '[t]ypically the man is successful in a particular social, cultural or professional milieu, married to a woman generally recognized as exemplary and acknowledged as such by her husband.' Ben Ali's first wife was in fact the daughter of a general and of good social standing. 'There may be children, and both parents have a caring, responsible attitude toward them' – which was the case, as the couple had three daughters. But, '[t]he man also has a mistress, usually of a different social, cultural or professional milieu' – here was Leila, if anything, a mere hairdresser. 'The women know about each other and appear to suffer under this situation, and there are multiple opportunities for public embarrassment as the man's involvement with both women impinges on his business, professional, social or political life. The man himself seems unhappy and distraught, oscillating between dedication to one woman or the other.'[7] This fits their situation to a tee. For a time both women lived in apartments in the Carthage palace; 'The period when the two women are neighbors and shared the presence of the head of state is terrible. Na'ima is an educated woman ... She suffers enormously from the situation.' The two women fought over issues like the organization of the cuisine, and Leila was reportedly jealous of Ben Ali's first wife.[8]

In such cases, the man may project a 'Madonna–prostitute' image onto his partners. This is a 'typical ... dichotomy from male adolescence', which may persist into adulthood and old age, and may be culturally reinforced in patriarchal societies where such 'double morality' is tolerated and even fostered.[9] According to experts, this 'Madonna–prostitute' image reflects a split view of the women, whereby one is socially accepted and the other is catalogued as a whore. This impression, earlier projected onto two women, his wife and Leila, respectively, constituted a conflict for the male partner. Ben Ali overcame it by legitimizing the relationship and bringing Leila into the palace as his lawfully wedded wife.

This certainly coheres with *vox populi*'s perception of their relationship. Leila has always been considered by the Tunisian people as of lower social stature than her husband, and as a woman who tried to compensate for it by earning a baccalaureate degree as well as her *maîtrise*, both through correspondence courses. Whether or not she actually received these diplomas is a hotly contested question.

'Tunisia, Inc.'

To what extent Leila Ben Ali Trabelsi actually manipulated her husband and became the real power behind the gigantic web of corrupt economic, financial, political and social enterprises will finally come to light in more detail as the post-revolution era unfolds. In addition to the few studies that have been published on the Ben Ali/Trabelsi clan, mainly outside the country to evade censorship, certainly official investigations will yield a more precise picture of how 'Tunisia, Inc.' – essentially a family enterprise – ran the entire country as a profit-making racket.[10]

There is no doubt that Leila Ben Ali was a – if not *the* – driving force behind this conglomerate. When her influence became dominating can only be surmised. Historians generally divide Ben Ali's presidency into three phases, from the early years after the coup in 1987, when he introduced political and economic reforms, to the period in the 1990s, when he brutally suppressed his internal Islamist opposition and expanded economic liberalization, to the new millennium, when he officially reinstated the life-time presidency and consolidated power through a party-state which was ruled as a police state.[11]

Phase One: The Coup

The bloodless coup occurred on 7 November 1987, during which Ben Ali, accompanied by a team of doctors dressed in surgical white, went to the presidential palace to announce to the senile 86-year-old President Habib Bourghiba that, due to his physical/mental incapacitation, they would escort him out of office. In his first official speech after the coup, Ben Ali declared that, in accordance with the constitution, the Prime Minister would take over temporarily and that was in fact the case. He also pledged far-reaching political reforms, most importantly, that the life-presidency would be abolished. 'The age we live in can afford neither a lifelong presidency nor automatic succession to the top position of the State, from which the people find themselves excluded. Our people deserve a developed and institutionalized political life, based on a multi-party system and pluralism.'[12] Deeds followed his promises, as a law passed the next year laid the formal grounds for a multi-party system with legal status for parties, and press laws relaxed earlier restrictions. In 1988 the life-presidency was officially abolished through a constitutional amendment, which limited the head of state to three terms of five years each and set an age limit of 70 years on that office.[13]

At the same time, Ben Ali introduced a slew of so-called economic reforms, which came down to drastic liberalization of the economy, including currency devaluation, cutting import tariffs, facilitating exports through tax breaks and relaxing price controls and exchange rates.[14] These were the reform mechanisms that would open up the economy to wholesale looting from foreign interests in cahoots with domestic mafias.

The manner in which the bloodless coup occurred merits closer consideration, for it was not a purely internal Tunisian development. On the contrary, the entire operation was conceived, planned and implemented by outside forces, to be precise, Italian intelligence, a fact which was to have far-reaching implications for Tunisia's relative independence in decision-making. The inside story of the coup remained secret until 1999 when Fulvio Martini, who had been the head of Italy's military intelligence (SISMI) for seven years, serving under the governments of Bettino Craxi, Amintore Fanfani, Giovanni Goria and Giulio Andreotti, revealed inside information in hearings at the Italian parliament. The hearings, organized by the Commission on Massacres which investigated various terrorist incidents that had plagued Italy, heard testimony for example on the 1978 kidnapping and murder of Prime Minister Aldo Moro by the Red Brigades.

In the course of Martini's explosive testimony, he suggested continuing behind closed doors, and it was under those conditions that the truth about Ben Ali's coup came to light. 'In the years 1985–1987,' he testified, 'we organized a kind of *coup d'état* in Tunisia, placing President Ben Ali as head of state, replacing Bourghiba who wanted to leave.' The political context was defined by the emergence of Islamist fundamentalism in Algeria, which the Italians feared could reach Tunisia. Bourghiba's response would have been violent repression which, they feared, would only lead to negative consequences there and in neighbouring countries. The Italians were concerned that any destabilization of Algeria and/or Tunisia could adversely affect the gas pipeline running from Algeria to Italy through Tunisia. In August 1983, on orders from Prime Minister Craxi and Foreign Minister Giulio Andreotti, Martini issued directives to 'his' people in Tunisia. 'We succeeded in concluding an initial transaction on the main points of disagreement,' he later reported, 'then we proposed a satisfactory solution for all which was accepted, and the succession after Bourghiba took place with a calm and peaceful transfer of power.'[15] Craxi himself flew to Algiers in November 1984 and urged the Algerians to be patient. Meanwhile he and his government were planning the coup against Bourghiba of 1987.

Phase Two

Ben Ali's second phase was marked by a turn toward political repression. This came first in response to the 13 per cent electoral gains by the Islamists in the 1989 elections, which sent a shock wave through the political establishment, a shock that was echoed by the Islamist (FIS) gains in Algeria's 1990 elections and the subsequent bloody civil war. Ben Ali responded with vicious repression of his domestic Islamists, which led to the exile of the opposition group Ennahda in 1992. Having crushed that perceived threat, Ben Ali won the staged 1994 presidential elections with a 99.44 per cent margin (he was the only candidate). Significantly, he staked his entire political legitimacy on promises of economic growth, which was a backhanded acknowledgement of the Islamists' appeal: job-creation, foreign investment, infrastructure development, along with greater political freedoms.[16]

But, instead of making good on these pledges, the regime exploited the worldwide reaction to the 11 September 2001 attacks in the US, to exert top-down political control. Just two weeks after the Twin Towers were hit, the ruling party Democratic Constitutional Rally (RCD) 'called on' Ben Ali to announce his candidacy for re-election, even though by law he should not have been allowed to run.

Phase Three

In the third phase, Ben Ali did officially reinstitute the life-presidency by holding a referendum in May 2002 which eliminated the constitutional barriers to his candidacy, and extended the age limit also to 75 years.[17] In this same period, Ben Ali consolidated his one-man rule and the party-state structure. He himself ruled as 'head of state, the head of government, and the head of the State Council, … the chairman of the ruling party, the commander-in-chief of the armed forces, and the head of the judiciary as well as the chairman of the constitutional council. The presidential palace became the command and control center for the country, and all major decisions were taken there by the head of state.'[18]

And the increasingly prominent figure in the palace, which was the command centre for all decision-making, was Leila Ben Ali Trabelsi. In the first phase she seems to have played no role at all, as would be fitting given that, although she was his mistress, he was still presenting himself as the head of a traditional household with wife and children. It was after his separation from his first wife that he shifted from pseudo-reformer to authoritarian, and following his marriage (1992) to Leila that he further tightened his presidential control. This is not to suggest a one-to-one causal connection, but merely to point out that Ben Ali, who had profiled himself as a reformer and had maintained a relatively low profile in his early years as president, seemed to undergo a personality change at the same time that his private life was entering a new phase. In his earlier years he was in fact a somewhat modest personality who did not seek publicity and whose public appearances were rare.

Leila Ben Ali Trabelsi was quite the opposite, at least following her legitimization through marriage to the president. Her primary concern, which took on the character of an obsession, was to establish a secure economic, political and social position, not only for herself but also for her family. It was as if the girl who had come from a poor family, and experienced the negative social consequences associated with this humble background, had taken a private oath not only to attain prominence but to become the supreme leader, the narcissist *par excellence*, who would be better, more beautiful, more powerful and more envied than anyone else. She knew exactly what she was doing. In 1970, she had told her sister-in-law Nadjia Djeridia: 'You will see, Nadjia, I will marry a prince, a king or a president. I will change your life, I will buy you houses. You will see, you will have maids and chauffeurs.'[19]

She seemed to have the wherewithal to reach her goals: 'She has other trump cards in her game: patience, intuition, manipulation, secrecy, intrigue, charm, seduction … Like her mother, the daughter is well versed in superstition, magic, evil and witchcraft.'[20]

Using all resources available to her, Leila moved ruthlessly to secure power in the long term. These resources included magic, which she took deadly seriously. One of her cooks revealed in a book published after the revolution that it was a daily ritual to burn a chameleon alive on a *kanoun*, a coal-fired grill. Leila gave him orders as to what he should do with the chameleon for the president: 'You will cut the chameleon's throat, put your finger into its blood and paint a circle around the ankle of the head of state, as if you made a *kholkhal,* [an anklet] but carefully, carefully, you must not leave any blank until the circle is closed!' The cook, who also obeyed orders to open the belly of the chameleon lengthwise, commented: 'However, I am obliged to state, that since the start of Leila's rituals, the president's will has been dwindling day by day. Imperceptibly, the relation of forces changes, moving to the other camp. Every time, Leila appeared stronger and more dominant. To her, nothing seems impossible. In exchange, the weakness of the president becomes more and more distinct.'[21]

This sort of will to power is the main motive for corrupt behaviour on the part of a political leader, who more often than not displays paranoia and anti-social traits.[22] And this is what the Tunisian First Lady did become. Together with her husband, she deployed her and his relatives and in-laws as functionaries of a vast national network encompassing all vital activities of a state and national economy. The 'extended family', as identified by Steffen Erdle, comprised the Ben Alis and the Trabelsis, plus all their relatives; the Trabelsis, meaning Leila and her siblings and their families; and the Materis, the family of Ben Ali's daughter Nesrine and her husband Mohamed Sakhr; plus the Shiboubs, Mabrouks and Zarrouks, whose family members married the daughters that Ben Ali had from his first wife. The entire network – about 60 families – numbered hundreds of individuals.[23]

Leila managed to organize affairs such that all the members of her extended family would be integrated into the spider's web of interlocking and interconnected enterprises in literally all areas of economic, social and political life in Tunisia. It is estimated that over 50 per cent of Tunisian enterprises were directly controlled by the network, known popularly as The Family or The Mafia. The Family controlled airlines, real estate, land, transportation, communications, banks, tourism, auto dealerships, media, agriculture and food processing, retail distribution, Internet providers and so on and so forth. There was virtually no sector of the Tunisian economy that was not managed by this network. And this includes emphatically the black market and 'informal' economy.

It was no less a man than the US Ambassador Robert F. Godec, who, in a series of cables to Washington from 23 June 2008, provided *prima facie* evidence of the existence of this monstrous mafioso operation in Tunisia. The summaries as published by WikiLeaks contain the following.

1. (S) According to Transparency International's annual survey and Embassy contacts' observations, corruption in Tunisia is getting worse. Whether it's cash, services, land, property or yes, even your yacht, president Ben Ali's family is rumoured to covet it and reportedly gets what it wants. Beyond the stories of the First Family's shady dealings, Tunisians report encountering low-level corruption as well in interaction with the police, customs, and a variety of government ministries. The economic impact is clear, with Tunisian investors – fearing the long arm of 'The Family' – foregoing new investments, keeping domestic investment rates low and unemployment high (Refs G,H) ...

2. (C) According to Transparency International's 2007 index, the perception is that corruption in Tunisia is getting worse ... When asked whether he thought corruption was better, worse or the same, XXXXXXXXXXXX exclaimed in exasperation, 'Of course, it's getting worse!' ... [H]e said that even the cost of bribes was up ...

3. (S) President Ben Ali's extended family is often cited as the nexus of Tunisian corruption: Often referred to as a quasi-mafia, an oblique mention of 'The Family' is enough to indicate which family you mean. Seemingly half of the Tunisian business community can claim a Ben Ali connection through marriage, and many of these relations are reported to have made the most of their lineage. Ben Ali's wife, Leila Ben Ali, and her extended family – the Trabelsis – provoke the greatest ire from Tunisians. Along with the numerous allegations of Trabelsi corruption are often barbs about their lack of education, low social status, and conspicuous consumption. While some of the complaints about the Trabelsi clan seem to emanate from a disdain for their nouveau riche inclinations, Tunisians also argue that the Trabelsis' strong arms tactics and flagrant abuse of the system make them easy to hate. Leila's brother Belhassen Trabelsi is the most notorious family members and is rumored to have been involved in a wide-range of corrupt schemes from the recent Banque de Tunisie board shakeup (Ref B) to property expropriation and extortion of bribes. Leaving the question of their progenitor aside, Belhassen Trabelsi's holdings are extensive and include an airline, several hotels, one of Tunisia's two private radio stations, car assembly plants, Ford distribution, a real estate development company, and the list goes on. (See Ref K for a more extensive list of his holdings.) Yet, Belhassen is only one of Leila's known siblings, each with their own children ...[24]

The last cables published by WikiLeaks are from 2009, and they contain oblique references to torture in Tunisian prisons, as well as direct reports of political corruption and lack of basic freedoms.

Leila's lifestyle was indeed scandalous in the eyes of the Tunisian people. The Sidi Dhrif palace, which she had built in Sidi Bou Said, was more a temple than a residence. The army was mobilized for its construction, which took five years, with workers labouring day and night. Several ministries were brought in to oversee specific tasks, the Agriculture Ministry, for example, which was responsible for planting trees. The massive structure housed a private clinic with top-notch medical equipment including facilities to provide for Ben Ali's chemotherapy treatments, and it was well staffed. 'The staff consists of two governesses, five cooks, two pastry cooks, three plumbers, six servants, two office clerks, sixteen chambermaids, three nannies, two electricians, five nurses, eight chauffeurs, 32 bodyguards, two swimming pool attendants, six gardeners and eight permanent painters.'[25] At a dinner to which the US ambassador was invited, the First Lady served 12 courses, composed of delicacies specially flown in from France. Only the chickens fed to the pet lion, named El-Materis, came from domestic production.[26]

True to her promise, Leila installed her family members in the palace beginning in 2002 and in 2005 bought them homes. At the same time, she broke ground in a new field: archaeology. With a fanatical obsession to possess art objects of great value, described as an 'addiction', she used her position to redraft zoning laws and expropriate sites with archaeological treasures, to loot the nation's artistic heritage.[27]

Leila also launched ostensibly charitable social activities, among them the Basma Association which she founded in 2000, to help find employment for the handicapped. In 2007, she oversaw the construction of the Carthage International School, built on land she received scot free from the government and financed by government money. As Ambassador Godec reported, Leila apparently sold the entire complex to a Belgian group, pocketing a net profit, since she had put no funds into the enterprise. She was also named head of the Arab Women's Association. Curiously, after the collapse of the house of Ben Ali references to these associations on the Internet were temporarily unavailable.

One particularly ostentatious and lucrative enterprise in 'women's affairs' was the Elyssa Club which she established as a private club only for women. Inspired by a similarly exclusive women's club which Suzanne Mubarak had invited her to visit, Leila pinched no pennies (of government funds) to build the club with facilities including 'a restaurant, a ball room, a movie theatre, a room for playing cards, another for playing chess, which was kept closed for lack of any players; a library which will never be visited, a casino, the kitchen and offices, one of them for Leila'.[28]

With these and other initiatives, Leila succeeded in passing herself off, at least outside Tunisia, as the prime mover for women's rights, which may have been a deliberate ruse to project an image of 'liberalism' in Tunisia as a way to counter reports of continuing human rights abuses.

The *Regent* book presents the convincing thesis that Ben Ali's regime introduced and consolidated 'state feminism' as a way of diverting international public opinion from the outrageous human rights violations being committed daily against the civilian population.

Leila led this feminist charge most aggressively and convincingly. She became the head of 'the Organization of Arab Women, the Centre of Arab Women for Promotion and Research, the national conferences of the National Union of Tunisian Women, the World Congress of Women Executives, the Basma Association for the promotion of the handicapped ...'[29] On the 20th anniversary of her husband's coup, she organized a conference on 'republican government and the role of women in the rooting of values and citizenship, and in reinforcing the development process'.[30]

Clearly, the Godmother of the Family was Leila Ben Ali Trabelsi, the one who 'inspired' and directed the operations, including those of her husband. Clinical studies on such narcissistic relationships have identified the phenomenon, noting that some 'narcissistic women, socially more successful, may actually identify fully with such idealized men, unconsciously experience themselves as the true inspiration of these men, and *may end up running their lives.*'[31]

Madame la Présidente

Leila ran the Tunisian presidency and the president, her husband Ben Ali. Exploiting the deteriorating health of her husband, she commandeered government figures to treat her as the boss. Beau and Graciet report on how Leila called in the closest advisors, Foreign Minister Abdelwaheb Abdallah, and the secretary general of the presidency, Abdel Aziz Ben Dhia, in a moment when Ben Ali was ill, and issued her marching orders: 'You know as well as I do that the president is going through a phase of depression because he exerted himself in service to the country. Therefore, I ask you be gentle with him, and avoid overloading him with news or dossiers which might worsen his condition. You can, in any case and on any subject, turn to me beforehand. I would know how to present things to him.'[32]

Here, Leila was issuing her directives to top government officials regarding general procedures she demanded be followed. She was the boss and should be briefed first and foremost. In addition, the actual day-to-day functioning of government affairs was in the hands of a network of so-called presidential advisors, about 40 in number, all faceless, who constituted a parallel government.[33]

The public perception and that of her immediate entourage was that the ageing and ailing president was increasingly ceding power to his ambitious wife. Suffering from cancer, Ben Ali strove to keep up appearances, dyeing his hair and consuming cocaine before chairing ministerial meetings. What he most enjoyed was spending time with his son and heir, Mohammad. 'For the time being, Leila rules,' his employees noted, adding, 'Several scenes made us think that the head of state suffers from a kind of senility that Leila plays with and enjoys.'[34]

Ben Ali on Stage

Although the general perception among Tunisians supported the view of the taxi driver that Ben Ali was controlled by his wife and the Family, this does not explain away or negate his own narcissism. He was born into a large and poor family, like Mubarak. His father was illiterate and worked at the harbour as a docker.[35] Ben Ali saw the military as the only option to make a career, and entered the army at the tender age of 15. Before coming under Leila's guidance, he had already asserted a pronounced tendency towards the desire for absolute power over others, in his having procured powerful positions in the military and intelligence realm. In late 1977 he assumed the post of National Security Director in the Interior Ministry and shortly thereafter put down a general strike of the UGTT union, which left 200 dead.[36] It should not be overlooked that when the bread riots broke out in 1984, Ben Ali was Secretary of State for National Defence and, two years later, Interior Minister. As ambassador to Poland in 1980, he had witnessed the brutal repression of the Solidarnosc movement and was to adopt similar methods against the Islamists as well as against the revolutionary movement in 2010.[37] Ben Ali made sure his own Interior Ministry would become a superministry, with a work force of 150,000 police – for a population of 10 million!

His establishment of a totalitarian dictatorship, enforced through police state methods, and guaranteeing his one-man rule, reflects the standard profile of a narcissistic leader, as seen in the cases of Qaddafi and Mubarak. When confronted by the popular upsurge in December 2010, even wife Leila could not shield him from the justified rage of a population that had been repressed and plundered for decades. Although never a charismatic speaker, and indeed more wont to stay out of the limelight, Ben Ali had to face his citizenry on 28 December.

In that first of three speeches, he displayed a variety of responses catalogued in the clinical literature. Referring to the tragic suicide of Mohammad Bouazizi which had ignited the mass protests, he was cold, hostile and detached from reality.

'While these events triggered by one social case,' he began, 'of which we understand the circumstances and psychological factors and whose consequences are regrettable, the exaggerated turn that these events have taken, as a result of their political manipulation by some sides who do not wish good to the homeland and resort to some foreign television channels which broadcast false and unchecked allegations and rely on dramatization, fabrication and defamation hostile to Tunisia, requires us to clarify some issues and confirm the truths that must be taken into consideration:

'First, we do understand the feelings of any unemployed person, particularly if his search for a job goes on, his social conditions are difficult and his psychological structure is fragile, which may lead him to resort to desperate solutions in order to draw attention to his situation.'

Ben Ali's depiction of Bouazizi's plight as 'one social case' of a person whose 'psychological structure is fragile' is a callous misrepresentation betraying his inability for empathy – as to be expected from a narcissist. Also typical of this psychological disorder, the Tunisian leader immediately sought scapegoats in the form of 'political manipulation by some sides' aided by the foreign press (i.e. AlJazeera television).

In appearing to address the real grievances of his people, Ben Ali noted unemployment, but quickly qualified that it is 'a major concern in the different countries of the world'. Tunisia, he went on, has a large number (80,000) of college graduates, a source of pride, and claimed, 'The State will strive to find solutions likely to meet job applications … [and] will act in the meantime to further increase wages and household incomes …' He offered no concrete measures to lend credibility to this promise and instead continued in his tirade against the presumed enemy:

> Consequently, there is no possible way … that we accept the exploitation of isolated cases, an event or fortuitous situation, to achieve petty political targets, at the detriment of the national

community's interests, its gains and achievements, first and foremost, concord, security and stability.

It is not acceptable that a minority of extremists and agitators in the pay of others, and against the country's interests, resort to violence and street disturbances as a means of expression ... This ... impedes the flow of investors and tourists which impacts negatively on job creation ...

Knowing, as the Tunisian people knew, that the real impediment to investment and job creation lay in the Family's mafia economy, his words could only ring false and cynical. After reasserting 'the need to respect freedom of opinion and speech' (following 23 years of brutal repression!), Ben Ali had the gall to conclude by saying, 'We are always committed to the social dimension of our development policy ...' Any objective viewer would have to conclude that the man was totally divorced from reality.

It was almost two weeks later that the Tunisian head of state managed to muster the psychological strength to address the public again, after daily demonstrations and countless casualties resulting from the use of brute force by his police. In that address on 10 January 2011 he reiterated in more emphatic and abusive terms his paranoid contention that it was outside agitators to blame. The 'violent incidents' were 'perpetrated by hooded gangs', who 'even assaulted citizens at home, in a terrorist act that cannot be tolerated'. The instigating 'parties', he charged, 'have not hesitated to engage our children', to 'incite violence', spreading lies and exploiting the suicide, 'an incident that we all regret.' Still, those responsible were 'a small group of hostile elements' acting out of 'jealousy for Tunisia's economic success story', 'ill-intentioned elements', 'hostile elements in the pay of foreigners, who have sold their souls to extremism and terrorism' and so forth. Making clear his intention to continue to respond with police violence, Ben Ali repeated, 'the law will have the last word. Yes, the law will have the last word.'

In these remarks, Ben Ali attempted to offer something concrete to redress the people's complaints, promising to 'double the capacity of employment', reaching 300,000 jobs by 2012, but it fell on deaf ears, given that he had promised the same thing over two decades earlier, and nothing had come of it.

Ben Ali concluded with hearty thanks to 'my dear Brother Leader Muammar Qaddafi, leader of the Libyan revolution', apparently for having welcomed Tunisian refugees who were fleeing the violence. Not coincidentally, it was to be Brother Muammar who would offer to provide him with aircraft to leave Tunisia.

His speech on 13 January struck a different note. First, the president appeared on television standing, whereas he previously had been seated behind his presidential desk. His body language showed he was agitated, his right hand and arm flailing this way and that, his voice rising at intervals.

The most significant feature of this, which was to prove to be his last speech, was his choice of idiom. Instead of speaking in classical high Arabic (al Fushaa), which he had championed since 1987, he announced that he was 'addressing his people in the language of all Tunisians'. Ben Ali had reintroduced the Fushaa in his very first speech following the coup against Bourghiba, who, as president, had spoken in various hybrid forms of Arabic or French, etc. Ben Ali resurrected Fushaa as the sole form of Arabic to be used in public addresses. If he did so at that time to signal the shift to a new era, now he was reverting to the popular idiom in a bid to establish communication with a population he had alienated for decades.[38]

From the standpoint of communications specialists, Ben Ali's adoption of dialect represented a desperate attempt to forge some link with his people. But he had lost all contact with reality, and could not see how far distanced from him his people were. In using dialect, he may have thought he was going on the offensive, but it did not work. According to one account, the idea of speaking in dialect had been cooked up by Leila.

So much for the form. As to content, Ben Ali's final speech combined attempts at expressing a human response to the dramatic developments with a hysterical insistence on familiar themes: that the violence was perpetuated by small groups, and that all Tunisians should come together for the good of the nation. He seemed to be pleading with his audience, repeating, 'I have understood you, I have understood you' and 'we have felt pain for the developments, a profound pain ... great sadness'. At the same time, he hammered away at the idea that it was small groups who were organizing violence, in what amounted to an immoral act, a crime, and called for national unity to defeat such groups.

Considering that he was speaking to the nation after almost three weeks of mass mobilization, during which 219 people had been killed and 510 wounded, and yet the numbers of demonstrators multiplied by the day to the eve of his speech, this can only be considered clinical denial. His people are telling him to leave office, and he calls for national unity against presumed grouplets fomenting division and violence!

Like Mubarak, Ben Ali tried to extol his 50 years of service to the nation, in military and political positions, in which he had made innumerable sacrifices. Like Mubarak, he said he was sad. 'My sadness is great, very great, and profound, very profound. That's enough violence! Enough violence!'

In his next breath, he announced that he had given the order to the police to stop using live ammunition against citizens, which was tantamount to admitting that that had been the case, and that, therefore, the deaths he pretended to regret and mourn had been provoked by his own police acting under his orders. What followed was a list of orders he had issued in hopes of saving the situation, although he must have known at that point that there was no exit. He announced the formation of an 'independent commission' to investigate the deaths, the introduction of press freedom for all media including the Internet, the assurance of freedom of political expression including through demonstrations (if lawfully registered), reinforcement of democracy and pluralism and so forth. His acceptance of demonstrations – with prior permits – smacks of true absurdity, considering that for two and a half weeks, the entire nation had taken to the streets against him, without the slightest consideration of a bureaucratic permit. Again, this is a sign of loss of touch with reality.

Ben Ali went on to unveil what he deemed were historic decisions – for example, that he would not run for president in 2014, and that thus, 'There will be no presidency for life. No presidency for life', he repeated in something of a daze.

The account of those last days in Tunis provided by his former employees is full of intriguing details that may or may not correspond to reality. One salient point presented is that Ben Ali had sought to appease the crowds and calm them down while Imed, Leila's nephew (perhaps actually her son), mobilized gangs of thugs to attack the demonstrators, thus escalating tensions. Ben Ali was livid and confronted him. He also confronted Leila, accusing her of being the cause of the uprising.

Suddenly, the head of state pushes Leila brutally:

• It's because of you! It's because of you! It's because of you!

Leila turns around and the insults get louder.

• Go …

Halima (Ben Ali's daughter) has just joined the group and shouts, in tears:

• Divorce, divorce, cut the contact to the Trabelsis! Put them all in prison, save your skin and save your people![39]

As the crisis deepened and it became clear that the end was near, Halima again urged Ben Ali to sacrifice the Trabelsis but he did not or could not. The same eyewitnesses report that Leila had pressured Ben Ali in his final speech *not* to mention the Trabelsi issue.

As the crowds rejoiced knowing Ben Ali's days were over, the family hastily prepared to flee. Ben Ali fell apart psychologically, refusing to enter the aircraft until urged to do so by security personnel. According to unconfirmed rumours, it had been provided by Brother Muammar and flew him to Saudi Arabia. Official accounts say he flew on the presidential plane. Not long after their announced arrival in Jedda, the news broke that Ben Ali had suffered a stroke and had been taken (under another name, to protect his security!) to a hospital. Whether or not the former president really suffered a stroke is beyond our ability to ascertain. But it is worth noting that, as the clinical literature documents, illness is very often a retreat from reality.

NOTES
—

1   Ben Hamida, Amor, *Chronik einer Revolution: Wie ein Gemüsehändler einen Präsidenten stürzt*, Books on Demand GmbH, Norderstedt, 2011, pp. 50–51.
2   http://dna-algerie.com/international/1164-les-lingots-de-leila-trabelsi-les-5-milliards-de-dollars-de-ben-ali-main-basse-sur-les-richesses-de-la-tunisie.html
3   Thomas Schmid, 'Tunesien: Die Jasmin-Revolution', in Frank Nordhausen, Thomas Schmid (Hg.), op. cit., pp. 33, 26. On 20 June 2011 Ben Ali and his wife were tried *in absentia* by a court in Tunis and found guilty of misappropriating public funds, sentenced to 35 years each, and fined US\$33 million and US\$26 million, respectively.
4   The biographical data are reported in Beau, Nicolas et Catherine Graciet, op. cit., p. 38, and Ben Chrouda, Lotfi, in collaboration with Isabelle Soares Boumalala, *Dans l'ombre de la reine*, Éditions Michel LaFon, Neuilly-sur-Seine Cedex, 2011, pp. 20, 22, 25.
5   Beau, ibid., p. 52.
6   Kernberg, Otto F. M.D., *Love Relations: Normality and Pathology*, Yale University Press, New Haven and London, 1995, p. 144. 'Most frequently, the narcissistic personality enacts his or her pathological grandiose self while projecting part of the self onto the partner, whose unending admiration confirms that grandiose self. Less often, the narcissistic personality projects the pathological grandiose self onto the partner and enacts a relationship between this grandiose self and its projected reflection. The partner in such cases is merely a vehicle for a relationship between aspects of the self. Typically, an idealized partner and an "appendix" or satellite to that ideal object constitute the couple in enactments or fantasy, or they form an unconscious 'reflection' in which each partner replicates the other. They can also, in complementing each other, jointly reconstitute a fantasied and lost grandiose ideal unit' (pp. 150–151).
7   Kernberg, op. cit., pp. 159–160.
8   Ben Chrouda, op. cit., pp. 29–30.
9   Kernberg, op. cit., p. 154.
10 Beau, Nicolas, op. cit.
11 Erdle, Steffen, *Ben Ali's 'New Tunisia' (1987–2009): A Case Study of Authoritarian Modernization in the Arab World*, Klaus Schwarz Verlag, Berlin, 2010, pp. 14–16.
12 Quoted in Erdle, ibid., pp. 94–95.
13 Erdle, p. 99.
14 Ibid., p.102.
15 Chianura, Carlo, 'L'Italia dietro il golpe in Tunisia' – L'ammiraglio Martini: Craxi e Andreotti ordinarono al Sismi di agire, *La Repubblica*, 10 October 1999.
16 Erdle, op. cit., p. 120. According to Beau and Graciet, the Islamist vote may have been as high as 30 per cent, op. cit., p. 25.
17 Ibid., p. 124.
18 Ibid., p. 136.
19 Ben Chrouda, op. cit., p. 19.
20 Beau, op. cit., p. 29. See also Ben Chrouda, op. cit., p. 40: Leila ordered sheep sacrifices when building projects were launched and p. 128, often roamed through cemeteries in disguise. For the relationships between magic among primitive

societies and in neurotics, see Freud's seminal study, *Totem and Taboo, Resemblances Between the Psychic Lives of Savages and Neurotics*, Random House, New York, 1918.

21 Ben Chrouda, pp. 15–18.

22 Kernberg, Otto F., *Ideologie, Konflikt und Führung: Psychoanalyse von Gruppenprozessen und Persönlichkeitsstruktur*, op. cit., p. 177.

23 Erdle, op. cit., p. 145–146, Beau, op. cit., pp. 41–46.

24 Wikileaks Cable: Tunisian Corruption and President Zine El-Abidine Ben Ali, http://middleeast.about.com/od/tunisia/a/tunisia-corruption-wikileaks.htm?p=1. See also Beau, op. cit., pp. 65–79 for details on family activities.

25 Ben Chrouda, op. cit., pp. 43–46.

26 Nordhausen, op. cit., p. 34.

27 Ben Chrouda, op. cit., p. 118.

28 Ibid., p. 132.

29 Beau, op. cit., p. 27.

30 Ibid., p. 28.

31 Kernberg, *Love Relations*, op. cit., p. 156, emphasis added.

32 Beau, op. cit., pp. 30–31.

33 Ibid., p. 59.

34 Ben Chrouda, op. cit., pp. 56–57.

35 Nordhausen, op. cit., p. 22.

36 Ibid.

37 Erdle, op. cit., p. 96.

38 Ben Ali speaks in Tunisian 'for the first time', http://languagelog.ldc.upenn.edu/nll/?p=2905). It is interesting to note that during the revolution, the demonstrators communicated in a wide variety of languages and dialects, not only Fuṣhaa and Tunisian dialect, but also French, English, and Spanish, Sonia Shiri, 'The Language of the Tunisian Revolution: Slogans, Tweets, and Facebook Posts', MESA conference, 3 December 2011.

39 Ben Chrouda, op. cit., p. 159.

5

Ali Abdullah Saleh: A Shakespearian Tragic Figure

For someone coming from a European cultural background, the spectacle of Yemen's President Ali Abdullah Saleh desperately asserting his claim to power and leadership conjures up images from some of Shakespeare's greatest works: King Lear on the heath who, having been stripped of his authority and entourage by his conniving daughters, desperately clings to his status. Or Richard III, who, facing enemies virtually alone on the battlefield, having lost even his horse, desperately calls for someone to provide him a steed: 'My kingdom for a horse!' he cries. And most relevant is the comparison to Hamlet, whose psychological inability to make a final decision and to act catalyses a series of tragedies.

The cultural context may be utterly foreign, but what makes the Shakespearian comparison credible is the fact that those tragic heroes, convinced they had been undone by plots and conspiracies, were ultimately themselves responsible for their fates. It was Lear's insane decision to divide his kingdom and Richard III's bloodthirsty lust for power that led to their doom.

And so it is with Yemen's would-be president-for-life; what led to the demonstrations calling for his removal beginning in January 2011 must be sought in his own policies and leadership style as president stretching back over 30 years. Saleh's biography, career and establishment of a political order bear striking similarities to the cases of Mubarak and Ben Ali and, consequently, his behaviour during the crisis echoed that of his North African neighbours. Although each is a distinct sovereign individual, all betray uncannily similar symptoms of personality disorders associated with narcissism, paranoia and hysteria.

From Poverty to Power

Like Qaddafi, Mubarak and Ben Ali, Ali Abdullah Saleh was born into a very poor family in Almaradh and, as a young boy equipped with not even a grammar school education, entered the military – the only opportunity to make something of himself. Just how young he was at the time is not clear, since there are two different dates given for his birth: his official biography gives 1946 but other sources say 1942.[1] If the former date is correct, then he was only 12 years old when he enrolled in 1958, which would make him a child-soldier according to current human rights categories. Even if he were born in 1942, he still would have been, at 16, a very young soldier. Wild stories have circulated on the Internet about Saleh's family background, some intimating that he was an illegitimate child, whose father abandoned the family. Official biographies say he was brought up by his stepfather Saleh, the brother of his deceased father, but details such as names of individual family members are lacking. Equally extravagant accounts exist regarding his leading role in the 1962 revolution and his suffering wounds in the civil war in 1963. Again, depending on his birth date, his age and rank at the time raise questions as to the veracity of such reports. Whatever the details, there is no doubt that Saleh grew up in dire circumstances and came to know the horrors of war at an early age.

Like Qaddafi and Mubarak, he rose rapidly in the military hierarchy and in July 1978 was elected President of the Yemen Arab Republic and Commander-in-Chief of the Armed Forces, re-elected in 1983. Following further promotions, to Field Marshal and General, he became President of the Presidential Council of united Yemen in May, 1990, and was re-elected in 1993, 1994 and 1999, the latter being the first direct presidential election. Unopposed, he won that election by 99.2 per cent. Meanwhile in 1999 the parliament had extended the presidential term from five to seven years and that of parliament from four to six years. Flanking the parliament was an advisory council with legislative powers, appointed by the president. In 2002, Saleh declared that he would not stand for re-election in 2006, but then, bowing to 'popular pressure', he did, and won by 77.2 per cent. His intention to run again after his term elapsed in 2013 was one of the factors that triggered the revolution in Yemen.

The Family

Ali Abdullah Saleh presents a good example of how power corrupts. Like Ben Ali and his wife Leila Trabelsi, Saleh reorganized the state as a family enterprise, perhaps as a psychological reaction to his irregular familial relations. He lent new meaning to the term nepotism: deriving from the Italian *nipote*, which means nephew, nepotism refers to the practice of conferring privileges on family members. Historically, it was often the case that a Pope who, as a celibate, could have no children, would treat his illegitimate offspring as 'nephews' and confer special privileges on them. Saleh has placed his nephews in top positions, and it is no wonder that the opposition demanding his resignation specified that his relatives – especially the nephews – be sent packing.

The distribution of power and privilege among the Saleh clan members is reminiscent of the Ben Ali/Trabelsi set-up, except that Yemen, unlike Tunisia, is dirt poor. So the enterprises, funds and institutions to be divvied up are perhaps less lucrative than those in Tunisia, although the principle and mechanics of corruption are the same. Depending on what sources one can access, the Saleh family power structure included his son, seven half-brothers, five nephews and 11 in-laws.[2] The posts they inherited were awesome: his son, Ahmed Ali Abdullah Saleh, was Commander of the Republican Guards (which counts 30,000 men) and the special forces. Three nephews, sons of his late brother and all colonels, occupied key security posts: Yahya Mohammed Abdullah Saleh was Chief of Staff of Central Security, which was said to control major cities including Sana'a, as well as Counterterrorism; Tareq Mohammed Abdullah Saleh was Commander of the Special Guards; and Ammar Mohammed Abdullah Saleh was Deputy Head of the National Security Agency. Another nephew, Tawfick Saleh Abdullah Saleh, chaired the National Tobacco and Matches Company. Yahya was also active in the economic sphere, in the Almass Company for Petroleum Services and the Chinese Ha Wi Cable Company.[3]

The half-brothers were military officials: Brigadier General Mohammed Saleh Al-Ahmar was Commander of the Air Force, Brigadier General Ali Saleh Al-Ahmar was Chief of Staff of the General Command; and Brigadier General Ali Mohsen Al-Ahmar, whose family relationship is not clear, commanded the First Tank Division and the North Western Military Zone. Other leading military posts were in the hands of members of Saleh's Hashed tribe and those who came from his Sanhan village.

Among the half-brothers and in-laws were captains of industry, holding executive positions in oil, engineering, agriculture, construction, transportation, infrastructure, pharmaceuticals and the like. As for the government, there were in-laws in the ministries of youth and sports, the foreign ministry, the ministry of planning and international co-operation, as well as the Presidential Palace and the diplomatic corps. And, to close the circle, the Saleh extended family is also intermarried with prominent families like the Bayt al-Qadi.

It is against this Yemeni version of the Trabelsi Family that the opposition in early 2011 rebelled. Following Saleh's failed attempt to alter the constitution which would have allowed himself yet another term in office, rumours had been circulating that, like Mubarak, he planned to have his son succeed him after 2013, when his term runs out, an option no one accepted. In its five-point plan for a transition of power, the Joint Meeting Parties (JMP) listed 30 names of people who must be removed, many of them noted above. Their first target was of course President Ali Abdullah Saleh, and he responded with the same crudeness displayed by those grandiose leaders in Tunis and Cairo. Speaking on television on 23 January, he arrogantly dismissed the succession rumours as 'utmost rudeness', and in the same breath announced raises in salaries of the armed forces, obviously to bolster their commitment to repress the demonstrators.

With top-down family control over the police, special forces and military, Saleh had no qualms about giving the orders to fire on civilians demonstrating peacefully. He said he had given such orders to the security forces 'only in cases of self-defence', but, since the demonstrators were unarmed, this was patently false. Included in the forces of repression were paid thugs and snipers, firing live ammunition from rooftops. The death toll in late February was over 12, and continued to rise day by day, reaching a climax on 18 March when 42 people died in an assault on the university, most of them from bullet wounds in the head and neck. It was this event, a 'massacre' according to one medic, that redefined the political context, and leading members of the establishment began to register their moral outrage by resigning. Saleh declared a state of emergency.

A Vacillating Narcissist

Saleh's behaviour, from the start of the protests and escalating in intensity, echoed that of Qaddafi in several aspects: he bolstered his own authority by organizing pro-government demonstrations, treated the opposition with utter contempt and sought refuge in conspiracy theories. In addition, he coquetted with his interlocutors in what looked like a cat-and-mouse game whose only function was to gain time, in hopes of staving off the inevitable. As each day passed, he progressively lost touch with reality.

The ostensibly 'pro-government' rallies gathered thousands on several occasions in the capital Sana'a; at first, participants were paid the equivalent of US$3 per day, plus food and a day's ration of Khat, Yemen's popular drug.[4] By the beginning of April, he was bussing crowds in from other cities, and the price according to press accounts had risen to US$250 for Sana'a residents, US$350 for others.[5] In a country where 40 per cent of the population lives on US$2 a day, that's a fortune. Carefully staged for state television camera and the foreign press, the rallies featured masses wildly cheering their leader and shouting, 'The people want Ali Abdullah Saleh!'

While bathing in the artificially orchestrated adulation of the masses, Saleh denounced the protesters as 'provocateurs'. On 21 March, he triumphantly declared, 'We're still here', and that the majority of the people supported him. 'Those who are calling for chaos, violence, hate and sabotage are only a tiny minority.' He told a crowd of supporters on 25 March, that his opponents were 'a tiny minority of drug dealers and money launderers', whose leaders were 'adventurers and conspirators who would seek to reach power over the dead bodies of martyrs and children'.[6]

Earlier he had officially accused the US and Israel of fomenting unrest in Yemen and the whole Arab world. 'There is an operations room in Tel Aviv with the aim of destabilizing the Arab world,' he said, and that central headquarters was 'run by the White House.' He added: 'Mr Obama, you are President of the United States and not of the Arab world.'[7] On 21 February, he had told the press, 'The arbiter is the people and not the American Embassy, the United States or the EU.'

When, after several top military figures shifted their support to the opposition, Saleh called them 'stupid', condemned their 'foolishness', and 'a reaction to what happened on Friday'. 'What happened on Friday' was a cruel euphemism for the university massacre, and in fact that did trigger several high-level defections. In the same speech, Saleh continued to entertain delusions of power, by offering the military defectors an 'amnesty' – as if he still had the means to prosecute them!

The same self-aggrandizement appeared in his repeated refrain, *'Après moi le déluge'*. In a meeting of 22 March, with the military still on his side, he threatened civil war: 'Those who want to climb to power through a coup,' he said (referring to the defectors), 'should know that things won't stabilize. The nation won't be stable, it will turn into a civil war, to a bloody war, so they should think carefully.' Days later, he told Al Arabiya television that he would not transfer power 'to chaos' – i.e. the opposition. On 26 March, he said 'Yemen is a ticking time bomb', and that if he were not on the scene, civil war would break out.

Conflict Inside the Mind

The most clinically interesting manifestation of his personality structure appeared in the cat-and-mouse game he tried to play with the opposition and the international community regarding possible diplomatic solutions to the crisis. It was not only a matter of Saleh's political manoeuvring, but also a reflection of a profound split inside his own mind.

The issue from the outset was clear: the opposition, which was initially made up of youth and students and developed into a broad-based movement representing all social layers, took to the streets to effect a regime change that they had never been able to achieve with their vote due to rigged elections. They insisted on political reforms, beginning with the exit of the current regime, Saleh and his family, to be followed by real elections. Saleh's first response, at the beginning of February, was that he would step down without seeking any dynastical succession, but would do so only at the end of his term in 2013. The two sides met at the beginning of March, during which the opposition, the Joint Meeting Parties, presented its five-point plan, pivoted on Saleh's giving up power by the end of 2011. On 5 March, the presidential office issued a statement to the effect that he would not budge until 2013. Two days earlier, Saleh insiders said there had been 'initial acceptance' of the plan, then later said it had only been 'favourably received'.

On 10 March, Saleh pledged in a speech to rewrite the constitution, to grant more powers to parliament. The constitution was to be drafted by a group of political and social figures, presumably of the president's choosing, and then presented to the people in a referendum. The opposition's response was summed up in one word: 'Leave, Mr Saleh. This is our demand.'

Following the defections of high-level military and diplomats, and the expansion of the opposition to include journalists, doctors and academics, on 21 March, according to a presidential spokesman Ahmed al-Sufi, Saleh told a meeting of tribal leaders, military brass and senior officials that he would leave office by the end of the year. Two days later, he issued a letter to the opposition groups, in which he proposed the new constitution with referendum, then elections all within 2011. In response to determined calls by the opposition that he vacate the presidency now, Saleh said, yes, fine, but … On 24 March, he pledged that he would step down, but would turn over power only to 'capable hands'. 'I will hand over power to safe hands,' he said, 'and not to malicious forces who conspire against the homeland.'

Twenty-four hours had not passed before a presidential spokesman officially denied reports that Saleh would leave. On 27 March, Saleh himself addressed the issue in a meeting with his General People's Congress (GPC) party leadership, and said: 'I could leave power … even in a few hours, on condition of maintaining respect and prestige. I have to take the country to safe shores … I'm holding on to power in order to hand it over peaceably,' he said. Then came reports from AlJazeera and elsewhere that Saleh, in a meeting with tribal leaders later that same day, had assured them that he would stay put until 2013! His ruling party quickly seconded this view, adding that in any case Saleh would remain head of the GPC. Other reports had it that Saleh might agree to leave in 2011 but demanded continued control over his party.

On 2 April, the opposition JMP offered Saleh a solid, rational proposal for peaceful transfer of power. According to their five-point plan, Saleh should hand over power to his vice president, who would revamp the various security agencies (National Security Agency, Central Security Forces and Republican Guards). He would then join with the JMP to set up a transitional national council, with representatives from all political groups, which would draft a new constitution. In the interim, a transitional national unity government could deal with immediate economic and political developments.

Days later, the Gulf Cooperation Council (GCC) presented its own initiative, which dovetailed with that of the JMP, in that it called for transfer of power to the vice president and a transitional leadership council with broad representation, which would manage affairs for three months and prepare elections.[8] Some reports said he accepted it the next day, but later events were to contradict this. Although this offer included guarantees for Saleh's *de facto* immunity, he publicly turned it down. Speaking on state television 8 April, he rejected it as a 'coup against democracy' and 'blatant interference in Yemeni affairs'. In response, the GCC foreign ministers, obviously not amused, met on 10 April and openly called for Saleh to transfer power to his vice president and pave the way for a transitional government.

On 11 April, *Antiwar.com* reported that Saleh endorsed the GCC proposal, but on condition that the transfer proceed in a 'constitutional manner'. With this formula he was saying that regime change could come only through elections and they, as was well known, were scheduled for 2014! The opposition opposed the GCC's offer of immunity, but that was a moot point, considering that Saleh had essentially nixed it.

Impatient with the president's wavering, the opposition set an ultimatum on 14 April, giving Saleh two weeks to relinquish power. The following day he delivered his answer in a short address to supporters. Slandering the opposition as a bunch of 'bandits' and 'liars', he proposed they enter a dialogue with him. 'We call on the opposition,' he said in Sana'a, 'to consult their consciences and come to dialogue and reach an agreement for the security and stability of the country.' (He also chastised the demonstrators for mixing the sexes in violation of religious norms, a charge that triggered a vigorous response with thousands of women taking to the streets in protest.)

The GCC did not give up, but renewed its efforts at a solution. Meeting in Riyadh on 17 April were the foreign ministers of the organization together with Yemeni opposition figures from the Common Forum, including a former foreign minister and four leaders of political parties. Their proposal entailed Saleh's vacating the presidency within 30 days, and delegating power to his vice president. It spoke of a national unity government and a presidential election within two months. Included in the plan was the ouster of three top security chiefs, all relatives, Ahmed Ali Abdullah Saleh, Ammar and Yahya. Most important for Saleh was that the GCC, with the agreement of the opposition, was offering him immunity from prosecution.

Saleh responded on 22 April with a conditional acceptance, the condition being that everything proceed 'within the framework of the Yemen constitution', i.e. that he continue in office until 2013. In announcing his answer, he again lashed out at his opponents calling them 'renegade and cowardly elements' and accusing them of hatching 'plots against freedom, democracy and political pluralism'. One day later, a presidential aide, Tariq Shami, informed AlJazeera that Saleh had 'agreed in full' to the GCC scheme if the opposition also endorsed it. But then, in an interview with the BBC only 24 hours later, he turned around again. 'Who shall I hand (power) over to – those who are trying to make a coup?' he asked. 'No, we will do it through ballot boxes and referendum. We'll invite international observers to monitor,' he promised.

The farce continued into the next month. On 6 May, a new GCC deal was to be signed by 15 representatives on either side, but at the last minute, Saleh backed out. Another date was set, 18 May, for representatives of the Yemeni state and the opposition to sign a GCC-brokered agreement. Saleh again balked, saying that although opposition parties' representatives would sign, that did not guarantee that the youth demonstrators in the streets would desist. GCC General Secretary Abdullatif al Zayani, understandably miffed, left Yemen angrily.

On 22 May, after the opposition representatives had put their signatures on the document, ambassadors of the GCC countries, the US and the EU gathered to take part in the signing ceremony which Saleh was to host. Instead, again, he refused. Speaking on state television, he explained his refusal by pointing to the fact that the signing had not taken place in his presence. At an army celebration, the Yemeni president said the deal was tantamount to a coup adding that if he were to sign it, then Al Qaida would take over his country.

As tensions escalated in Yemen between Saleh's remaining forces and the militia led by Sadeq al Ahmar, head of the Hashid tribal confederation, in confrontations that threatened to degenerate into civil war, Saleh again signalled his readiness to sign an agreement along the lines of the GCC deal. Again, nothing came of the promise.

The conflict reached a climax on 3 June, when Saleh's headquarters were bombed, leaving him with massive injuries and extensive burns. He fled to Saudi Arabia for medical treatment. While lying in intensive care he sent messages announcing his imminent return to Sana'a, where the opposition ranks were swelling. On 19 June, clerics and tribal leaders united to issue a petition demanding the incapacitated Saleh's removal and new elections. Among the 100 signatories was the country's most prominent cleric, Sheikh Abdul-Majid Al-Zindani, leader of the Islamic party Islah. At the same time, masses poured into the streets to call for the expulsion of Saleh's son and nephews, who had stepped into the president's place, from the country.

In his first television appearance after the assassination attempt, Saleh declared his willingness to share power 'within the framework of the constitution' – i.e. again indicating his intention to stay on until 2013. Following eight rounds of major surgery in Riyadh, Saleh returned to Yemen on 23 September, allegedly 'carrying the dove of peace and the olive branch'.[9] His promises of a ceasefire were translated into escalated armed attacks against opposition forces, leaving 100 dead. His solemn pledge, yet again, to implement the GCC peace plan was a cruel lie.

The farce dragged on for months, while casualties were mounting in the deepening conflict. On 8 October, Saleh intimated that he could leave office within days, but 24 hours later, government representatives declared that their foreign minister was in the United Arab Emirates to propose yet another plan. In a speech delivered on 5 November, Saleh articulated a formulation that was as verbose as it was vague: 'We stress our intention to continue to support the efforts that Vice President Abd-Rabbu Mansour Hadi is undertaking in light of his mandate to complete a dialogue with the opposition and sign the Gulf initiative and its operational mechanism … to achieve a legitimate, peaceful, and democratic transition and conduct early presidential elections.' Interviewed by France24 on 14 November, the Yemeni leader swore he would step down within 90 days of the signing of the GCC accord. 'I know the difficulties, the negatives, the positives,' he said. 'I will not hang onto power.' And he added in what might be termed a Freudian slip: 'Whoever hangs onto power I think is crazy.' In clinical analysis such an utterance actually amounts to dissociated material suddenly surfacing without the person's realizing its connection to his behaviour or statements. Could Saleh, in his thirst for power, ever think that he might be crazy?

One may discuss the merits and demerits of the proposals tendered to end the crisis, but that is not the point. As the record shows, President Saleh was psychologically neither able nor willing to address the offers rationally. Had he been able to, he would have weighed the pros and cons and decided that, so long as his vital interests – his physical and mental well-being, and security (including immunity) – were protected, it would be advisable to resign his post in dignity and seek a future elsewhere. That is what the GCC's very generous offer would have guaranteed him, but his psychological mind-set could not accept it.

In the estimation of professional psychiatrists, the president's Hamlet-like vacillation was more than a time-buying tactic. As he subjectively experienced it, the situation was continually changing, and certain parts of his personality were in conflict with other parts. Imprisoned by this internal split, he was literally incapable of making a decision.[10] Then, as if by surprise, on 23 November, he finally put his signature at the bottom of the deal the GCC had hammered out, which mandated the transfer of power within 30 days to the vice president in exchange for immunity for himself and his family. Immense political pressure especially by the US and the Saudis had come down upon him to make the decisive step. Yet even a signature on the dotted line did not guarantee that he had made that step. For, Saleh demanded and was given the right to retain the title of 'honorary president' during the transition. At face value, this would appear to be a ludicrous concession, granted merely to honour the continuing clinical denial on the part of the Yemeni president. From a psychological standpoint it made it possible for Saleh to keep the fantasy of power alive. But, at the same time, he apparently fought to translate the fantasy into reality. As Nobel Peace Prize winner Tawakul Karman denounced in an interview to the *Frankfurter Allgemeine Zeitung* on 10 December, the same Saleh who had signed the agreement to cede power was still holding on and continuing to rule through a vice president who deferred to him for any decision. She charged that the transitional national unity government being put into place was made up 50 per cent of representatives of the 'corrupt regime', and called for the military and security branches to be put under an independent commission. In addition, Saleh's family members clung to their posts in defiance of the demands made by the revolution – for as long as they could.

'Every Inch a King!'

A most remarkable feature of Saleh's behaviour during the revolution was his refusal to acknowledge that he was losing grip, and that his entire power apparatus was crumbling before his eyes. Thanks to psychological defence mechanisms, he was able to simply deny that any of this was happening.

It began in late February when representatives of the Hashid and Baqil tribes distanced themselves from Saleh, himself a member of the Hashid. Following the 18 March university massacre, the Minister of Tourism resigned, along with Yemen's ambassador to Lebanon and the deputy education minister. It was at this point that Saleh fired his entire cabinet, perhaps as a pre-emptive measure since he knew they were about to resign *en masse*. Seven more ambassadors resigned on 21 March, including Yemen's man in all-important Saudi Arabia. Days later, the ambassador to the UN left, along with ministers for human rights, religious affairs and the director of the SABA news agency. On 21 March, it is reported that five Yemeni ambassadors to Europe had resigned, those accredited in France, Belgium, Switzerland, Germany and Great Britain, as well as those in Jordan, Syria and Cuba. At the same time, Major General Ali Mohsen Saleh defected along with a general and commanders of three regions, dealing the regime a potentially mortal blow. The news that Sheikh Abdul-Majid al-Zindani, the cleric and politician, had thrown his support behind the protesters must have delivered a further shock. There followed in short order the resignation of the representative to the Arab League Abdel-Malik Mansour.

In mid-April a group of senior officers joined the cheering protesters. They included members of the Air Force, the Central Security, and the Republican Guard. Days later on 18 April AlJazeera broke the story of a new political party having been formed by members of the ruling party. Among those creating the new organization that supported the opposition were three ex-government officials, the former Transport Minister Khalid al Wazit, former Tourism Minister Nabil al Faqih and former Human Rights Minister Huda al Ban, and 20 former parliamentarians of the General People's Congress party.

Day after day, Ali Abdullah Saleh, President of the Republic of Yemen, had to wake up to the news that again hundreds of thousands of citizens were gathering in Sana'a and other cities calling for his dismissal, and that his ambassadors to the most influential countries were pulling out their support.

Tribal leader Sadeq al Ahmar put it most poetically when he said that Saleh would 'leave this country barefoot' – i.e. bereft of any social or political support. As it turned out, Saleh was forced to flee the country in even more dire circumstances following the 3 June assassination attempt, perhaps not barefoot, but with no more than the skin on his back, and much of it severely burned.

In his first short televised message in early July following his retreat for medical care, he appeared with a headscarf to cover his wounds, desperately attempting to present himself still as the Yemeni leader. There was Saleh, in faraway Riyadh, like King Lear on the heath in the midst of a storm of biblical proportions; not only totally stripped of all royal trappings, ermine robes, crown and what-not, Lear had also lost his entourage – his security troops, palace guard, everyone. His daughters had cut his following from 100 to 50, from 50 to 25, then down to one. The only thing he had left was his delusion of power and grandeur, that he was 'every inch a king', a delusion that his faithful servant Kent held up. Although Lear had long since lost all political power and was on the way to losing his wits, the loyal Kent reassured him that he was the king, addressing him ceremoniously as 'Your majesty'.

Some die-hard loyalists in Sana'a, after seeing their leader battered and burned on television, quietly hailed the appearance of the president. And when he returned to the Yemeni capital, they took up arms in a last-ditch attempt to prop up his position as 'the Head of State'. In the end, Saleh could console himself with the thought that, after all, even after having signed the GCC agreement, he still retained the title of 'honorary president', did he not? And after seeking exile in the US in late January 2012, albeit under the pretext of medical treatment, he still clung to the promise that he would return to Yemen.

NOTES

—

1   His official biography is available at http://www.yemen-nic.net/English%20 site/SITE%20CONTAINTS/presedency/President/Biog.pres.htm, the National Information Centre of Yemen (French) at http://www.yemen-nic.info/fr_site/ President, and http://www.presidentsaleh.gov.ye/ in Arabic.

2   *The New York Times*, 5 January 2010, 'In Yemen, US Faces Leader Who Puts Family First; Ali Abdullah Saleh Family in Govt and Business', http://armiesofliberation. com/archives/2006/04/08/ali-abdullah-saleh-family-in-yemen-govt-and-business, http://arabrevolution.posterous.com/updated-full-list-of-ali-saleh-family-relativ, and http://commentmideast.com/2011/04/yemen-a-family-business/; Dresch, Paul, *A History of Modern Yemen*, Cambridge University Press, 2000, 2002, pp. 149, 189, 201–202.

3   Significantly, Saleh's nepotism goes back to his first years in office. In the late 1970s, his half-brother Ali Saleh was responsible for Hizyaz, 'the gate of Sanhan', later head of the Republican Guard, and his full brother Mohammad Abdullah Saleh was Chief of Central Security, Dresch, ibid., p. 149.

4   *Frankfurter Allgemeine Zeitung* (*FAZ*), 2 March 2011.

5   *Asharq Al-Awsat*, 1 April 2011.

6   *FAZ*, 26 March 2011.

7   Ibid., 2 March, *TIME*, 14 March 2011. *The New York Times* reported in March that Saleh called Washington to transmit his 'regret for misunderstandings' about the remarks.

8   The rational and generous proposal drafted by the GCC was summarized by *Asharq Al-Awsat* on 22 April 2011.

9   It was widely mooted in the international press that some *quid pro quo* had been arranged between the US and Saleh to allow his return. The deal allegedly involved Saleh's providing intelligence leading to the location and assassination by drones of Yemeni-American Anwar al-Awlaki on 30 September, followed two weeks later by the killing of his son. *The New York Times* wrote on 9 October: 'Mr Saleh's government has made much of its role in providing the United States with the critical intelligence on the whereabouts of the American-born cleric Anwar al-Awlaki, enabling the CIA to kill him in a drone strike at the end of September.'

10 Saleh has been described by US diplomats, in remarks published by WikiLeaks, as a 'wily, irreverent and sometimes erratic Yemeni autocrat'. That he is erratic is documented in his constantly changing attitude in the crisis. That he is 'wily' can be surmised from reports of his duplicitous behaviour with regard to his US relations. Thus, for example, in discussions with General David H. Petraeus following US missile attacks against Al Qaida sites in Yemen, Saleh emphasized that his official line was that these were not American but Yemeni air strikes. 'We'll continue saying the bombs are ours, not yours,' he pledged. And if American munitions were discovered at the sites, then the Yemenis would simply say, well this was old equipment we bought from the US.

6

Bashar al-Assad: The Great Pretender

'If you want to talk about Tunisia and Egypt, we are outside of this; at the end we are not Tunisians and we are not Egyptians ...' This is how Syrian President Bashar al-Assad put it in an interview with *The Wall Street Journal* on 30 January 2011, two weeks after Zine El-Abidine Ben Ali had fled Tunisia for Saudi Arabia and two weeks before Egyptian President Hosni Mubarak would resign and seek refuge in Sharm al Sheikh. He attributed the uprisings in both countries to 'desperation' on the part of the Arab population, desperation about economic ills as well as the failure of the regional peace process. But Syria, he repeated, was different. 'We have more difficult circumstances than most of the Arab countries,' he elaborated, probably alluding to hostility from the US to his country's foreign alliances, 'but in spite of that Syria is stable. Why? Because you have to be very closely linked to the beliefs of the people. This is the core issue. When there is divergence between your policy and the people's beliefs and interests, you will have this vacuum that creates disturbance.'

A month and a half later, the revolutionary tide swept Syria's shores, as small protests broke out in Damascus and Daraa. On 18 March, security forces fired on demonstrators, killing three, in what was the opening salvo of a confrontation that was to escalate over the subsequent weeks and months into the following year. The conflict can be divided into roughly four phases: from the onset in March to June; from June to the end of the year; from January 2012 to July; and from late summer on. Initially, Bashar could have dealt politically with the non-violent opposition but the violent response advocated by the hardliners around his brother Maher, head of the Presidential Guards, prevailed. The leadership complex will be examined below; suffice it to say here that as president, Bashar had the power to act otherwise, but did not and therefore can be held accountable.

From a psychological standpoint, Bashar's responses exhibited several patterns: his published statements occurred either as speeches to select audiences (parliament, government, the university) or interviews to international media; these appearances were separated by long periods of silence, up to four months at a time, which may reflect a 'narcissistic avoidance,' a tendency to avoid conflictual situations; he denied facts on the ground and shied away from personal responsibility; he increasingly fixated on formalistic definitions rather than addressing substantial issues.

The first phase opened with peaceful demonstrations, including protests against mistreatment of children in Daraa who had scrawled anti-government slogans on walls. Initially, citizens called on President Assad to implement promised reforms and only after the confrontation turned violent and casualties mounted in Daraa, Hama and Jisr al-Shoughour, did they demand his ouster.

Bashar al-Assad addressed the crisis three times in the initial phase, always in meetings with selected audiences which were broadcast on state television. At the end of March, after a prolonged silence (for which he apologized), he told members of Parliament it was a conspiracy, 'part of the continued conspiracy against this country'; he said he was sure that his countrymen knew that 'Syria is facing a great conspiracy whose tentacles extend to some nearby countries and far-away countries, with some inside the country'. Rejecting the term 'revolution' as inappropriate, he said the conspirators had 'mixed up three things: sedition, reform and daily needs', and that since sedition had taken the lead, many well-meaning people calling for reforms had been misled. 'They will say that we believe in the conspiracy theory. In fact there is no conspiracy theory,' he quipped. 'There is a conspiracy.' To Syrian ears this was more than plausible, given the history of plots and coups that the country had experienced.

His speech was interrupted repeatedly by approving applause, words of praise and poems recited impromptu by members of Parliament, and he joined in the antics. Why did Assad appear to be swept up in the process, clapping his hands in a frenzy and making jokes accompanied by hysterical laughter while citizens were being shot in cold blood and mourners, marching to bury their dead, were targeted by snipers? Professional psychiatric opinion reads this as an uncontrolled reaction to the enormous pressure created by the violent confrontations, a sort of safety valve which prompted him to laugh when the more appropriate emotional response would have been to weep.

In Assad's reference to reforms, he hinted at the conventional explanation offered for his failure to implement them: 'Many officials, particularly foreign officials,' he said, 'tell me that they think that the president is a reformer but those around him restrain him. I tell them that on the contrary the people around me are pushing me hard to do these reforms. What I want to say is that there are no obstacles, there are simply delays.'

Before examining this crucial point about reform in more detail, it is important to review Bashar's second major speech, a fortnight later. In the interim the protests had been expanding and the response of the security units as well as gangs of pro-government thugs (Shabiha) had only gained in violence. When 27 demonstrators were killed in Daraa on 8 April, the official news agency SANA put out the line that 19 members of security ('martyrs') had been killed by 'armed groups which use live ammunition'. By 11 April, more than 200 had died, according to a letter sent by the Damascus Declaration group to the Arab League, which called for sanctions against a regime that it accused of continuing to guard Hafez al-Assad's legacy.

Muntaha al-Atrash, the well-known human rights activist and daughter of the Commander of the Syrian Revolution Sultan Pasha al-Atrash, refuted the conspiracy theory and offered Assad the sound advice that he resign and return to practise medicine.

The president had named Agriculture Minister Adel Safar as prime minister with the task of putting together a new government. It was to this new government that Bashar al-Assad spoke on 16 April. Again, he had taken his time. The content and thrust of the speech represented a 180-degree shift from his earlier address. Here, instead of conspiracies it was reforms, reforms, reforms. Only in one connection did he address the conspiracy issue, this time completely redefining its role. Referring back to the first speech, he stated:

> There is the conspiracy. There are the reforms and the needs. The conspiracy has always been there as long as Syria acted independently and as long as it has taken its decisions in a way that does not appeal to many parties. And as long as there are adversaries or enemies, conspiracies are natural around us. That's why we *shouldn't* give this component a lot of attention. What's important for us is to focus our attention on strengthening our internal immunity inside Syria. (emphasis added)

Accordingly, he listed reforms and corresponding promises and pledges: he would lift the state of emergency and replace it with new legislation regulating the 'process of demonstrating', which might necessitate restructuring of the police; the government 'should start to study' a law on political parties; new laws on local administration and on the media would also be on the agenda. Not only does Syria need reforms, he emphasized, but also they must be implemented, and within specified timeframes. Turning to economic issues, Bashar acknowledged the people's justified calls for infrastructure and especially for jobs. He offered projects to provide employment in agriculture as well as industry, in the private as well as public sectors.

Though artfully crafted, the speech fell short of the mark for two reasons: first, because while he was speaking the regime's police and thugs were still roaming the streets. In fact, their violence would reach unheard of heights on 22 April through Easter Sunday, in what became known as the Good Friday massacre, killing somewhere between 80 and 120. Second, because he had been saying these things for his 11 years in office. In fact, many concepts and proposals echoed those he made in his inaugural speech in 2000.

Following the holiday violence, the regime deployed tanks and thousands of troops to the city of Daraa where the first protests had broken out. In a carefully prepared onslaught, they cut electricity, water and mobile phone communications before moving into the city militarily. Snipers perched on rooftops were reportedly 'firing at everybody' and 18 people died, bringing the death toll to an estimated 300 since the outbreak of the crisis. The Mufti from Daraa, Resk Abdulrahman Abaseid, resigned in protest, as did 233 members of the ruling Ba'ath Party. Analysts began to predict the disintegration of the regime, while international pressure on Damascus to refrain from force grew.

From April to May the conflict escalated in Daraa, spreading to Latakia, Douma, Homs, Baniya and Kafr Shams, with the same *modus operandi*: army units on tanks would encircle and occupy a city after having cut utilities (electricity, telephones and water) and fire indiscriminately on protesters. By the end of May, an estimated 1,000 Syrians had been killed and about 10,000 arrested. Prisoners who were later released spoke of vicious torture.

Continuing sieges of civilian areas climaxed in Jisr al-Shoughour near the Turkish border, where soldiers who refused to follow orders to fire on citizens were reportedly executed and defecting soldiers as well as civilians sought refuge in hastily erected camps in Turkey.

The news of Jisr al-Shoughour, retaken by the military on 12 June, sparked international protests by Turkish Prime Minister Tayyip Erdogan and UN Secretary General Ban Ki Moon.

On 20 June, with an estimated 1,400 dead, Bashar al-Assad finally re-emerged into public view. If his first speech denounced the conspiracy, and the second promised reforms, this address at Damascus University combined the two. 'I don't think there has been a single day,' he said, 'when Syria has not been the target of plotting, whether that be for geopolitical reasons or because of its political positions.' Those conspiring against his country, he said, were divided into three groups: peaceful demonstrators with legitimate grievances, 'outlaws and [those] wanted for various criminal cases' and extremists.

After denouncing the extremists he turned to the reform agenda, promising parliamentary elections for August, with new electoral and local administrative laws. A commission was to report its recommendations regarding the constitution, which might entail changing Article 8, which gave the Ba'ath Party a monopoly.

In order to establish this 'new political reality', in which the citizenry would soon control the state and hold officials accountable, Bashar announced the creation of a new institution, the 'national dialogue', which would guide the reform process.

Interspersed in his address were tell-tale admissions testifying to his increasing psychological insecurity. Right at the onset he had to account for his notable absence in the lengthy period that had elapsed since his second public appearance. He admitted that 'it took me some time to address you', and explained that this had been due to his concern not 'to make my speech a platform for propaganda' about pledges rather than achievements. Instead, he wanted his speech to reflect the countless discussions that he said he had held with citizens in the intervening period. 'Credibility after all,' he intoned, 'has been the foundation of my relationship with the Syrian people, a relationship built on deeds rather than words and on substance rather than form.' The significance of such an uttering will become clear in our psychoanalytical examination of Bashar's political performance in office.

Another hint of psychological uncertainty came in his reference to 'rumours' about him and his family that had been spread during his absence from the political scene. Such rumours (which he left undefined) were, he said, untrue.

Finally, Bashar addressed the issue of his personal, political role and responsibility in the process. 'When some people say,' he stated, 'that the president should lead the reform process, this does not mean that he can replace the people and carry out the reform process on his own. Leadership does not mean that one individual should stand alone but rather he should be in front and the people proceed with him. Leadership is a process of consultation and interaction.' What did he mean by this? That he, the president of the nation, was not in a position to determine a reform course?

The popular response to Bashar's university of Damascus speech was to return to the streets. Demonstrations broke out also in the refugee camps. Again, he was promising 'reforms' with no substance, announcing the formation of 'committees' and 'commissions' without any indication of who would join them or how they would be appointed. Students demonstrating in Aleppo called the president 'a liar', the psychoanalytical significance of which will be discussed below.

Taking the Media by Storm

Following his 20 June performance, Bashar al-Assad went into hibernation and remerged some four months later. In the closing days of October he ventured out to face world public opinion, this time in a concerted effort to project a sanitized version of events and an idealized image of his person through a carefully orchestrated media barrage. Major interviews appeared in *The Daily Telegraph*, Rossiya TV and *The Sunday Times*. He even graced American television with his presence on ABC.

In the interim, the crisis had taken a dramatic turn for the worse, as the expanding crackdown by military and police translated into rising daily casualty tolls, with no sign that the protesters would desist. The city of Hama became the symbol for the resistance – Hama, where in 1982 Bashar's father had ordered troops to open fire on members of the Muslim Brotherhood, leading to a death toll somewhere between 5,000 and 35,000. Hama, the saying goes, is the place where under the ashes, the embers are still glowing. The offensive began on 2 August, the beginning of the holy month of Ramadan, with tanks rolling into the city to occupy it, while snipers assumed positions on rooftops. Unofficial estimates of deaths reported by eyewitnesses numbered between 40 and 50 each day.

The opposition had meanwhile organized itself politically as well as militarily. In mid-September, a plethora of separate groups joined ranks in the Syrian National Council (SNC), which convened outside the country (in Turkey and Egypt) and began establishing rapport with foreign governments. Although the protesters at street level had maintained a principled commitment to non-violent resistance, soldiers and officers who refused orders to shoot civilians gradually banded together in a make-shift force, first to defend citizens, then to wage armed struggle against the regime. By November, the Free Syrian Army (FSA) launched its first armed assaults on military installations. Both the SNC and FSA were to function as foreign assets.

Syria was isolated, under political and economic pressure internationally, and rapidly gaining the status of a pariah state. The Syrian leader had ignored several options, from a peace plan forged by the Arab League (and Turkey), to mediation offers by Russia. Repeatedly, Bashar 'agreed' to Arab League timetables and repeatedly, he let them pass without event. Sanctions voted up by the EU, together with unilateral US sanctions, were putting the squeeze on the economy, but Damascus held firm. Russia led opposition in the UN Security Council to a resolution condemning Syria, and wielded its power of veto to prevent a repetition of the vote which had facilitated the deadly NATO war against Libya.

By October/November, the scenarios being publicly aired by think tanks, governments and the press ranged from a peaceful solution achieved through dialogue, to a military *coup d'état* or a palace coup against Bashar, as the first step in a process of gradual regime change and representative government, to civil war. The final alternative, civil war with sectarian dimensions and catastrophic regional repercussions, was clearly the worst-case scenario but not the least likely. Russian Foreign Minister Sergei Lavrov was the first to utter the term publicly in early November.

With the political noose tightening around his neck, Bashar responded with a press offensive. On 29 October, *The Daily Telegraph* published his first interview with a major Western paper since the onset of the Arab upheavals and his first public appearance since the 20 June speech. Bashar repeated almost verbatim his claim to *The Wall Street Journal* back in January 2011 that 'Syria is different in every respect from Egypt, Tunisia, Yemen. The history is different. The politics are different.' This time he followed up his broad claim with a threat: 'Syria is the hub now in this region. It is the fault line, and if you play with the ground you will cause an earthquake … Do you want to see another Afghanistan, or tens of Afghanistans?' he asked. 'Any problem in Syria,' he warned, 'will burn the whole region. If the plan is to divide Syria, that is to divide the whole region.' Regarding casualties, he said only 'terrorists' were being targeted.

His next assertion was either a conscious lie or a delusional fantasy. Distancing himself from other Arab leaders, he said: 'We didn't go down the road of stubborn government. Six days after [the protests began] I commenced reform. People were sceptical that the reforms were an opiate for the people, but when we started announcing the reforms, the problems started decreasing. This is when the tide started to turn. This is when people started supporting the government.' And the reforms were moving apace.

In his interview with Russian television, broadcast on 30 October, Bashar stressed that outside forces would refrain from attacking his country because they were aware of the consequences. Syria is unique, he said, geographically, geopolitically and historically; it is where two 'tectonic plates' meet, and destabilizing them would produce an earthquake affecting the region and the world. Bashar expressed his gratitude to Russia for having vetoed Security Council action, adding that he was 'counting on the Russian stance and continued support' to weather the storm.

Bashar's media barrage continued with a major splash in *The Sunday Times* on 20 November, also picked up by Russian television. The political points he made were nothing new: in fact, the primary thrust of the press campaign was not to make political points. It was to project a PR image of himself as anything but a ruthless leader. The *Times* journalist cast him in the following image: 'He could have been mistaken for a young business executive. Indeed, it was hard to imagine that the beaming figure in the dark suit who greeted staff warmly as he carried his own bags into the Tishreen palace was anything else.' She referenced 'the mild manner of the softly spoken leader', adding, 'he shook my hand with a smile, led me into a living room for tea and, having been briefed beforehand that my husband was ill, inquired solicitously about his health. "Have faith," he said, gently.'

With such gestures, Bashar placed the dialogue on a personal, quasi intimate level. The *Times* interviewer wrote: 'I asked him how he felt as a father – he has two sons, aged nine and six, and a daughter, aged eight – when he saw images of innocent children caught in the conflict.' His answer: 'Like any other Syrian, when I see my country's sons bleeding, of course I feel pain and sorrow. Each spilt drop of blood concerns me personally.' Again, when she inquired what he would say to mothers who had lost children, he answered: 'Naturally, as a father, I sympathize with [them],' adding that he had met with victims' families. She wanted to know if his children had seen pictures of the dead on television, and asked for explanations. Bashar: 'Unfortunately, they do and you have to explain it to them.' Affecting the posture of one who was morally affected by all the suffering, Bashar issued a firm pledge: 'My role as president – this is my daily obsession now – is to know how to stop this bloodshed caused by armed terrorist acts ...' And, yet, curiously, this 'obsession' did not disturb him emotionally. His emotions seemed split from events. 'I am naturally calm,' he commented. 'I do not deal with crises emotionally. I deal with them calmly. This makes me more productive and more capable of finding solutions. Stress is negative.'

Also in his *Telegraph* interview, Bashar had presented himself as the normal, regular guy, in stark contrast to the narcissistic strongmen from Mubarak to Qaddafi. Interviewer Andrew Gilligan described the unusual setting of their talk in Damascus:

> When you go to see an Arab ruler, you expect vast, over-the-top palaces, battalions of guards, ring after ring of security checks and massive, deadening protocol. You expect to wait hours in return for a few stilted minutes in a gilded reception room, surrounded by officials, flunkies and state TV cameras. You expect a monologue, not a conversation. Bashar al-Assad, the president of Syria, was quite different.
>
> The young woman who arranged the meeting picked me up in her own car. We drove for ten minutes, then turned along what looked like a little-used side road through the bushes. There was no visible security, not even a gate, just a man dressed like a janitor, standing by a hut. We drove straight up to a single-storey building the size of a largish suburban bungalow. The president was waiting in the hall to meet us.
>
> We sat, just the three of us, on leather sofas in Assad's small study. The president was wearing jeans. It was Friday, the main protest day in Syria: the first Friday since the death of Colonel Qaddafi had sunk in. But the man in the centre of it all, the man they wanted to destroy, looked pretty relaxed.

Bashar described his daily life as a way of explaining his immense popularity. 'The first component of popular legitimacy,' he said, 'is your personal life. It is very important how you live. I live a normal life. I drive my own car, we have neighbours. I take my kids to school. That's why I am popular.'

The media blitz culminated in a television interview with none other than Barbara Walters on ABC, broadcast on 7 December. The Syrian president appeared much less sure of himself, and came across as someone under extreme psychological pressure. His stated intent was to get American media to 'tell the truth'. His mode of expression was less fluent than usual, and at times he uttered self-contradictory statements as if he had lost the thread of his thought. In responding to questions, he fixated on definitions in a compulsive manner. For example, when Walters said Syria was isolated, he responded: 'That depends on how you describe, or how do you define isolation and support? ... How do you define isolation? If you don't define it, it's just a term.'

As for content, he reiterated several points made earlier: the reforms were underway with a series of new laws introduced; the majority of the Syrian people supported him; among the protesters were extremists, terrorists and convicted criminals; Syria was the fault line in the region, etc. Most startling was his detachment from personal responsibility:

Walters: Do you think that your forces cracked down too hard?

Assad: They are not my forces, they are military forces belong to the government.

Walters: OK, but you are the government.

Assad: I don't own them. I am president. I don't own the country, so they are not my forces.

Walters: No, but you have to give the order?

Assad: No, no, no. We have, in the constitution, in the law, the mission of the institution to protect the people to stand against any chaos or any terrorists, that their job, according to the constitution ...'

     ...

Walters: You gave – but who gave the order to react against the protests?

Assad: You don't need order, because this is their job.

The most tell-tale remark Assad made, presumably inadvertently, was a denial of the intent to kill. 'OK, we don't kill our people, nobody kill[s],' he declared. 'No government in the world kill[s] its people, unless it's led by a crazy person.' Reminiscent of Saleh's blurting out the thought that anyone who clings to power is crazy, this too appears to be dissociated material erupting without Bashar realizing the implications of his words.

The Syrian Civil War

In 2012 a third phase in the Syrian drama opened, in which the UN, the Red Cross and others would openly speak of 'civil war' and international efforts at mediation would take shape, first through former UN Secretary General Kofi Annan, then by Algerian diplomat Lakhdar Brahimi. The FSA enjoyed military, financial and political support of the West, via Saudi Arabia and Qatar, and a host of armed groups ranging from isolated mujahideen volunteers to organized bands of Al Qaida terrorists increasingly swelled its ranks. Supplied with sophisticated heavy weaponry, the combined military insurgency (albeit not under unified command) moved to the offensive, beginning in early spring to target Damascus and Aleppo, and armed conflict raged in these and other urban centers despite the presence of UN monitors. Both sides engaged in atrocities in a conflict which was assuming ethnic, religious and sectarian connotations. An inflection point was reached on 18 July, when military crisis staff members, including Bashar's brother-in-law and deputy chief of staff Assef Shaukat, as well as the former and current defense ministers, were killed by a bomb in the national security headquarters in Damascus. As the violence ravaged major cities, refugee flows expanded throughout the year, displacing up to 1.5 million internally and sending almost 500,000 to camps in Lebanon, Jordan and especially Turkey. As Turkish authorities officially embraced the rebellion, tensions with Syria rose, with cross-border shelling and the downing of Turkish aircraft.

As 2012 neared its end, a further shift occurred: those international forces (the US, Europeans, Saudis, Qatar and Turkey) which had hijacked the protest movement and hoped to steer it, each according to its own perceived interests, found themselves at odds regarding the composition of those fighting on the ground. If the Saudi and allied elements consciously promoted their ideological co-thinkers among the jihadists, the West, led by the US, struggled to separate the most unsavory terrorist components from what it strove to present as a 'legitimate' resistance force. As winter set in, the US would scramble to assemble a 'new' political opposition with a veneer of respectability, so as to allow Western governments to accord it some form of 'recognition'. This fourth phase bore the marks of an overt geostrategic confrontation, pitting the anti-Assad front and its international sponsors against the Syrian regime and its allies (Russia, China, Iran, Hezbollah). Options for NATO to support Turkey with Patriot missiles were rushed through, along with overt threats of international military intervention should Syria cross the 'red line' and deploy chemical weapons.

Throughout 2012, Bashar al-Assad made periodic public appearances. The first was at Damascus University on 10 January, after which he vanished for four months. In the summer he granted five interviews before absenting himself again for two months. In November he resurfaced in the Russian press. Obvious security concerns would explain this pattern of disappearances, but, from a psychological standpoint, there may also be a factor of conflict avoidance involved. That is, this personality type tends to avoid confrontational situations and, when making appearances, exhibit a splitting between his own positive personal self-image and the regime hardliner's violent handling of the crisis.

In his lengthy address at the university, the Syrian leader hammered away at several themes which he was to repeat in his encounters with journalists. Again, the conspiracy and reforms were leading issues, but now with a markedly different accent. Following public exposure of foreign backing for the FSA, Bashar could assert that 'external conspiring is no longer a secret because what is being plotted in the pal talk rooms has started to be clearly revealed before the eyes of the people'. Given the role assumed by the Arab League in expelling Syria as a member and joining in sanctions, he could argue that that organization had betrayed the Arab cause and, in contrast to its perfidy, hail Syria's principled stance and achievements. 'Has the Arab League ... returned one olive tree uprooted by Israel or prevented the demolition of one Palestinian house in occupied Arab Palestine?' he asked. In contrast, 'Who, more than Syria, has offered to the Palestinian cause in particular?'

Regarding reforms, he stated that implementing them 'will not prevent terrorists from being terrorists' and had nothing to do with the crisis but reiterated that he had maintained his commitment to political reform as 'the natural context': 'That is why we announced a phased reform in the year 2000'. 'Whether we were late' or 'Why we were late is a different question'. The measures he said he had introduced included lifting the state of emergency, issuing a political parties law and a local administration law, to prepare elections. The only measure which had been delayed was the anti-corruption law. As for the constitution, he had issued a decree to establish a committee which was working on it.

Bashar opened his summer press campaign with an interview to Rossiya-24 TV on 16 May, followed by discussions with Iranian channel 4 TV on 28 June, the Turkish paper *Cumhuriyet* on 3 July and German national television (ARD) on 8 July. His only reported encounter with Syrian institutions was a brief cabinet meeting on 26 June, in which he stated: 'We live in a real state of war from all angles'. The main point he stressed in his Russian television appearance was that the support Russia and China had lent was not to the regime but to 'international stability' and that it was motivated by their understanding of the geopolitical situation in the region.

In discussion with Iranian TV, he underscored his approval of Kofi Annan's six-point plan for a ceasefire, at a point in time just prior to the former UN Secretary General's admission of failure. Although Bashar repeatedly endorsed the plan for a ceasefire and negotiated political solution, his government made no moves to implement it. The rest of the interview focused on the theme of Syria's role as leader of the Arab resistance, introduced in his university presentation. The conflict in Syria, he said, was between resistance (against hegemony) and the New Middle East project, which was as old as colonialism. And Syria was paying the price for its policies, especially its defense of the Palestinian cause. Again, he asserted that the reform process had been ongoing since 2000 and that 'even if we implemented reform now or before, what happened would have happened, because it was planned abroad and not a spontaneous issue linked to reform'. He dealt at length with the Al Qaida factor as a 'US creation financed by Arab countries'.

His encounter with Turkish journalists focused on relations between the two countries, strained in the wake of Syria's downing a Turkish plane in late June. Bashar played it down as an 'accident', which could have been avoided had communication between Ankara and Damascus been normal. But, since 'we are in a state of war', Syria had to assume it was enemy aircraft. Again, he endorsed Kofi Annan's view that the crisis should be settled inside Syria, adding that sovereignty and non-interference into the country's internal affairs remained paramount.

Just days later Bashar al-Assad received Jürgen Todenhöfer, the veteran German journalist who had consistently sought to counter the anti-regime press propaganda. Bashar reiterated his support for the Annan plan, 'a very good plan which should not fail', just when its author was bowing out. In this, as in his other summer interviews, Bashar seemed preoccupied with definitions of terms in a formalistic fashion. Already in his January university address, he had objected to the term, 'national unity government' on grounds that, since 'we do not have a national division', there could be no need for such a unity government. Queried about the 'opposition', he had answered by saying, 'the opposition is usually an institutional body which is established by elections' but at present, 'we do not have elections; so how do we define the opposition?' He argued similarly in his German ARD interview: 'For me, the mechanism is the elections. If you represent the people, you go to the election, you run the election and you win seats, you can come to the government. While if you're only opposition – you don't have any seat in the parliament – whom do you represent? Yourself?' When asked whether or not he would leave office, Bashar told Todenhöfer, 'If I don't have a support in the public, how could I stay in this position?' He said that his people did want reforms, but the majority did not demonstrate for them. He told the Turkish press that it was not the office that counted, but his achievement. The height of equivocation came in his exchange with ARD regarding those responsible for civilian casualties:

Todenhöfer:	So you say that rebels, whom you called terrorists, have killed more civilians than the security forces?
Assad:	Not really. They killed more security and soldiers maybe than civilians – I talk about the supporters.
Todenhöfer:	But if we only talk about the civilians, did the rebels kill more civilians than the security forces? Or did the security forces kill more civilians?
Assad:	That's what I mean. If you talk about the supporters of the government – the victims from the security and the army – are more than the civilians.

On 18 July, as noted, a bomb exploded in Damascus, killing Bashar's brother-in-law, Assef Shaukat. Although initially attributed to the FSA,

another view was that Shaukat and his crisis staff were meeting to discuss a negotiated deal with some opposition figures, and regime hardliners who opposed it planted the explosives. In September, Shaukat's wife Bushra left Syria for Dubai citing differences with her brother on strategy and fears for her safety due to a 'quasi-coup taking place' within the leadership. Whoever was behind the attentat, it marked a turning point. With the exception of a terse written statement issued on Armed Forces Day (1 August), and a brief showing at a mosque on 19 August, Bashar was absent. On 29 August he gave an interview to a Syrian television outlet, Al Addounia, which seemed defensive. Asked about the escalation in Aleppo and Damascus, Bashar stressed that 'the situation is practically better but resolution hasn't been achieved and this takes time'. The military could have crushed the enemy in Homs, but such 'operations take time'. The questions themselves were of special interest, as they touched on sensitive issues inside Syria; 'there are those among the opposition,' the interviewer asked, 'who talk and ask why the Syrian forces and the Syrian army are inside Syrian cities, while not a single bullet has been fired on the Golan for nearly forty years,' to which Bashar replied: 'The task of the army and the armed forces in all countries of the world is to protect the homeland.' What followed – as reported on the official presidential website – sounded incoherent:

> President Al-Assad: … Syria adopts the ideas of resistance. But the other idea is that if Syria adopts resistance, then why isn't there resistance towards the Golan – this may be the idea you mean – then resistance is emerges [sic] when a state abandons its responsibility in reclaiming its land, which didn't happen in Syria like in Lebanon, maybe because of the civil war at the time, and like in Palestine where there's no state in the first place to reclaim rights, so the resistance had to exist. When we abandon, as a creed, policy and armed forces our primary goal of reclaiming land, then there will be a Syrian resistance.

He was also asked about 'those who say that the popular movement in Syria remained peaceful for four or five months and became armed after it was oppressed by the state' and replied that 'the main goal was rallying the people by shooting protesters, security men and the police so that the police and security respond and kill more civilians; thereby spreading a state of hostility against the state'. As for the growing number of defections, Assad returned to definitions:

President Al-Assad: … But let us examine the term. First, defection is when one establishment separates from a bigger establishment that presides over it or the defection of a part of an establishment from the main establishment, and at the top of this establishment is an individual or individuals who rebel against the higher levels or the main establishment. This didn't happen. What happened was that individuals who were occupied certain positions fled the country, which is a process of desertion and escape, not defection … In the end, those who flee are either weak or bad, because a patriotic and good person doesn't runaway and doesn't flee abroad. Practically, this process is positive and a process of self-cleansing of the state first and the country in general, so we mustn't be upset by this process because it's positive.

Another two months passed before Assad came into public view, this time on Rossiya-24 TV. Although he continued to focus on definitions – of 'civil war', for example, which he denied existed in Syria – his main message was that the war was against 'terrorism and instability' and had nothing to do with personalities like himself. Given the arms smuggling and massive outside support for the insurgency, he predicted it would be a long-term war. From the psychological viewpoint, the most salient features included his reluctance to entertain the possibility of having erred.

RT: What is your biggest mistake?

BA: I do not now remember to be frank. But I always, even before taking the decision, consider that part of it will be wrong but you cannot tell about your mistakes now. Sometimes, especially during crisis, you do not see what is right and what is wrong until you overcome the situation that you are in. I would not be objective to talk about mistakes now because we [are] still in the middle of the crisis.

RT: So, you do not have any regrets yet?

BA: Not now. When everything is clear, you can talk about your mistakes, and definitely you have made mistakes and that is normal.

RT: If today was March 15, 2011, that is when the protest started to escalate and grow, what would you do differently?

BA: I would do what I did on March 15.

RT: Exactly the same?

BA: Exactly the same: ask different parties to have dialogue and stand against terrorists because that is how it started. It did not start as marches: the umbrella or the cover was the marches, but within those marches you had militants who started shooting civilians and the army at the same time. Maybe on the tactical level, you could have done something different but as a president you are not tactical, you always take the decision on a strategic level which is something different.

And, whether knowingly or not, the Syrian president echoed his Libyan counterpart when he announced, 'I have to live in Syria and die in Syria.'

As I write it is impossible to predict the outcome of the Syrian crisis. Throughout 2012 Bashar presented no new options and the opportunity for dialogue with a non-violent opposition had passed, while civil war raged and neighboring countries (Lebanon and Turkey) became involved. The political, logistical and financial interference of the Qatari-Saudi-Western alliance against Damascus consolidated the geopolitical conflict with potentially devastating global implications. It also bolstered Bashar's charges that an international conspiracy was afoot.[1]

The Bashar Enigma

The crisis that erupted in March 2011 thrust onto centre stage a paradoxical enigma which had plagued Bashar's leadership since his inauguration, and which demanded resolution. Put simply, the question is: was Bashar really the modernizing reformer that he and others, including in the international community, put forward? Were his concerted efforts at reform being systematically blocked by an 'old guard' reluctant to give up its privileges? Or was Bashar his father's son, following the same agenda and wielding the raw power of the same institutional instruments established in the authoritarian dictatorship through which Hafiz al-Assad had ruled for three decades? Was he merely adopting the trappings of a reformer in order to mask his commitment to perpetuate his father's legacy? Did he, as one dissident put it, just represent a 'modernized authoritarianism'?

The bloody events of the revolution that erupted in 2011 would seem superficially to support the latter hypothesis: for, contrary to the pledges to reform and democratize public life, the government responded with force to demonstrators who were demanding just that. Significantly, in the early stages of the revolt, protestors seemed to be asking for the implementation of the president's promised agenda, and only after suffering casualties, shifted towards calls for his removal. They began to view him as an oppressor.

But how did the establishment succeed in cementing a diametrically opposite image? If the persona that was projected to the Syrian and international public of a mild-mannered, future-oriented reformer was to have any credibility and enjoy any durability, it would have to cohere with the actual psychological makeup of the man. In short, it would be impossible to sell Bashar's new image to the world unless the image were to 'fit', so to speak.

This raises the fundamental question: what psychological personality structure can adequately describe the profile of the young president? Clearly, he displays none of the outward signs of personality disorders encountered in the other four leaders considered here. Bashar is not obsessed with asserting his own grandiosity, demanding attention and approval or indulging in exhibitionism à la Qaddafi. He seems to fulfil none of the prerequisites to be classified as a narcissist, a paranoid or a hysteric. Quite the contrary: for David W. Lesch, who published a biography of Bashar based on extensive personal interviews, the new Syrian president 'is basically a principled man. He is very unassuming, his laugh that of an innocent young man.' One is struck by his 'sincerity', and the fact that '[h]is personality, on the surface, has not been tarnished by power and position … He is, at heart, an honest and sincere man.' Lesch openly states, 'I believe he is essentially a morally sound individual …' What impresses people are 'his politeness, his humility, and his simplicity'.[2]

One of Bashar's friends told the biographer that 'Bashar could eliminate almost anyone in the country, but he chooses not to operate in that fashion. He sees himself as the compassionate healer, not the political assassin. The thuggish behaviour that is so commonplace in the region and was associated with his father is not in Bashar's character …' In fact, the reason why Bashar had decided to study medicine and especially ophthalmology was that 'he liked the healing side' of the specialization. While a student, he was popular among his classmates and displayed a 'caring, jovial bedside manner' with his patients that won him admiration.[3] Bashar is also portrayed as the ideal husband and father, one who would get up in the middle of the night to deal with a crying infant, would change diapers and gave his son daily baths for the first year of his life.

One could hardly dream of a more ideal personality to lead a nation. But then during his tenure as president, the authoritarian dictatorship set up by his father continued to rule. True, at the onset Bashar unveiled a new political course, and Syrian political figures and civil society activists who took him at his word seized the opportunity to launch open debate in Syrian society. But the 'Damascus spring' was short-lived, and by February 2001, winter had set in.

To Be or Not to Be a Successor

The Bashar enigma begins with his ascension to power in 2000. Two versions of the event and the process leading up to it have dominated political commentary of modern Syria. One holds that Bashar, following the death of his elder brother Basil in 1994, was brought into the role of crown prince and after six and a half years of intensive grooming, took over after Hafiz al-Assad's death. The other version claims that there was nothing of the sort, and that neither father nor son had any such succession scenario in mind. It just happened to work out that way.

I was in Amman in January 1994, just after the news had broken of Basil's untimely death in an automobile accident. My visit was due to an interview I had managed to arrange, after months of telephone calls and faxes, with Prince Hassan bin Talal, at the time Crown Prince of Jordan. While I was waiting in the antechamber for the meeting, Prince Hassan's secretary, a bright, well-educated young woman from an aristocratic family, expressed her dismay and compassion about the young Assad's death. 'Imagine how terrible it must be,' she said, 'for a father, the head of state, to lose his first-born son who had been destined to take over. What will Hafiz al-Assad do now?' The implicit message in her words reflected a central tenet of oligarchical thinking: of course dynastic succession must be observed. What other options are there?

And indeed, it came to pass that Bashar had to step into his brother's shoes. He immediately left London where he had been working as a resident at the Western Eye Hospital, a department of Imperial College Healthcare NHS Trust, continuing his studies in ophthalmology while serving as a trainee and collaborating in eye surgery twice a week.[4] According to one account, 'When he returned to Damascus, "Dr Bashar" was informed by his father that he would replace his brother.' He initially refused, but then his 'grief-stricken father would not take "no" for an answer …'[5]

He quickly enrolled in military training and became a tank battalion commander in November of that year, then rose to the post of major in January 1995. A year later, he entered the command and general staff course at the Higher Military Academy, and graduated in July 1997 with honours. Immediately thereafter he rose to the rank of lieutenant-colonel and assumed leadership of the Republican Guard brigade which Basil had commanded. In 1999 he became staff colonel. In parallel he acquired a political education, working closely with his father out of an office in the presidential palace, learning the ins and outs of domestic politics and, in the last two years before taking power, studying foreign policy.[6] His father sent him abroad on diplomatic missions to Europe and the Arab world, thrusting him into the public eye 'so that he would not be a total unknown when his father died'.[7] And he rose in the echelons of political power with meteoric speed. Not one day had passed after the senior Assad's death than Vice President Abdul Halim Khaddam, acting as interim president, promulgated the news that Bashar was now commander of the country's armed forces as well as general (fariq), 'the most senior military rank, which only Hafiz al-Assad had held'. The Ba'ath Party elected him secretary-general in mid-June, which paved the way for his becoming president. To do this legally, the constitution had to be changed, since it set a minimum age of 40 for candidates to that office, and Bashar was only 34. The National Assembly set to work and rushed through the necessary amendments. A referendum on 10 July confirmed Bashar's candidacy with a whopping 97.3 per cent, and not long after, he delivered his inaugural speech. Hafiz al-Assad had died on 10 June and on 17 July Bashar officially took power.[8]

A smoother succession would be difficult to imagine, which suggests that it had been carefully prepared and planned, perhaps years earlier. In fact, Bashar had begun to appear in public alongside regime leaders like Defence Minister Mustafa Tlas as early as 1994, and in that same year, his father started removing anyone in a position of power who opposed his son's succession. Major General 'Ali Haydar, chief of the special forces, was axed in 1994 and a year later Major General 'Adnan Makhlouf, who was commander of the Republican Guard, was 'resigned' due to tensions with Bashar. The Makhloufs were in-laws, relatives of Hafiz al-Assad's wife, who had carved out a large niche in the establishment, both politically and economically.[9]

A well-orchestrated public relations campaign prepared Bashar's inauguration to the presidency, beginning shortly after his brother's death. For a full year following Basil's demise, his father made sure that Basil's image appeared throughout the country, then, on the first anniversary of his passing, a different image appeared in public places. This was the 'new trinity', a poster with pictures of Hafiz, Basil and Bashar with the captions, 'our leader, our ideal, and our hope' respectively.[10] The implication was obvious, even to the uninitiated. At the same time Bashar assumed the image of public servant, leading an 'anti-corruption' campaign at the end of the 1990s, and posed as the man who would lead Syria into the 21st century with his commitment to development of the IT sector, as symbolized by his chairmanship of the Syrian Computer Society. Bashar contributed actively to cultivating these images. In an interview with Lesch, he explained his decision to enter politics in 1994 as the fulfilment of a 'family code' according to which one should 'always be for the public and always feel for the people'.

In short: the succession was prepared, carefully, efficiently and well in advance, and all went according to the script. But the Assad regime denies this most vociferously. Lesch, who visited Damascus in 2004 for three weeks for his numerous thorough-going interviews with Bashar, argues that there was absolutely nothing planned and that none of the major actors in the succession, neither father nor son, had anticipated anything. In one interview, Bashar told him:

> I never expected to be president. It was mentioned in the press and magazines everywhere but I never thought about it. He [Hafiz] never mentioned it or tried to push me to be president. I wanted to work in the public domain and I was a member of the [Ba'ath] party, but I did not expect to lead the party. He did not plan for me to lead the party; if so, he could have arranged that much earlier. There was a party conference already scheduled to be held the next week [the first such party congress meeting in fifteen years], and they wanted to cancel it, but I said no, and at the conference I was elected as head of the party. He [Hafiz al-Asad] never tried to get me to do anything presidential. It was my ambition to work in the public domain. But he never prepared me to be president.[11]

In the same exchange, Bashar presented a picture of his father as utterly uninterested in his son's possible political future. When Hafiz asked him why he entered the military after his brother's death, Bashar explained:

> I went back in because I was a military doctor. My father told me, 'Are you going back to London?' and I said 'No'. Then he asked me what I was now going to do, I told him that I am military now, and in the military you have the right to change specialties, such as toward engineering or officer school. For weeks he said that I can go back to London or stay in Syria as a doctor, but I said I wanted to go into the military, and eventually he was convinced of this and he said OK ...[12]

Significantly, at the height of the security crisis when Bashar appeared on ABC with Barbara Walters, he again told the tale that his father 'never spoke' to him about politics, and urged him to return to London, but the party, under pro-Bashar support from the people, wanted him and he 'nominated' himself.

To bolster this version, biographer Lesch cites an interview given by Hafiz al-Assad to French television in the late 1990s, in which he disavowed the very notion of dynastic succession:

> I am not preparing my son to take my place, nor have I ever heard him speak of this matter. It seems to me that the fact that such a possibility is mentioned derives from his activity, which earns him the esteem and love of his colleagues, as well as respect among the residents of the country. As for the issue of succession, there is no clause whatsoever in our constitution that gives the right of succession to family members.[13]

In 1992, *TIME* asked Hafiz al-Assad the same question, to which he simply replied: 'I have no successor. The successor is decided by all those institutions, state and constitutional organizations and party institutions. These, I believe, have deep roots because they have a twenty or twenty-two years long experience, and they are able to cope with this prospect.'[14]

There is also an interesting psychological insight to these accounts by Hafiz provided in an interview with Farouk al-Sharaa, a veteran foreign minister, who said he did not think Hafiz was grooming Bashar. The reason he gave points to Hafiz's own psychological disorders: 'So I do not think he was very enthusiastic to see his son replacing him,' he said, 'simply because perhaps he never thought he was going to die.'[15]

The accounts given by Hafiz al-Assad and his son, which biographer Lesch swallowed hook, line and sinker, obviously do not correspond to the truth, as established by the public record. And the deception continued into the Bashar presidency.

The Reformer Without Reforms

When Bashar inherited the presidency, he also inherited the authoritarian state apparatus his father had built, with its security and intelligence units, its military, bureaucracy, party and press institutions. In this respect, he was not much different from Mubarak, who took over after Sadat's death. And the apparatus that Hafiz bequeathed his son did not pale in comparison. The party functioned as a driving force for the regime's power and its interrelationship with the military established a 'Ba'athization of the army', or an 'army-party symbiosis', which guaranteed a prominent role for the military.[16] The security apparatus, understood as the Mukhabarat and the army, constituted the real basis of power, and the former, with its vast network of informants, ran affairs particularly outside the capital.[17] Assad had pursued secularization of public life, and an economic policy aimed at reforming rural areas and developing the middle class. But the system rested on the central role of the president, à la Nasser, with bodies like the National Assembly (or parliament) and the National Progressive Front (a coalition of allowed political parties *de facto* subservient to the Ba'ath Party) functioning like so many fig leaves to project the aura of democracy. The rulers under Hafiz were a small circle of intimates made up of military, intelligence and diplomatic personnel, with or without family links, who constituted the inner core of policy-making.[18]

Like Mubarak and his predecessors Nasser and Sadat, Hafiz al-Assad also cultivated the public image of an all-powerful figure, one who should arouse in the citizenry feelings of admiration, caution, awe and, of course, loyalty. Hafiz 'ordered state media to praise his regime regularly – telling them to compare him to Syria's national hero by terming him "the new Saladin" … Hafez also arranged for demonstrations on his own behalf.'[19]

Bashar rejected this personality cult very publicly, ordering on 17 July 2000 that the press cease referring to his late father as the 'immortal president' and more broadly avoid glorification of the office.[20] The new young president reduced public exposure of his own image. He also hated ritual adulation of his father, for example, in the practice of applauding in a public event each time the leader's name was mentioned, and he never came across as the son of a state president.[21]

Enter Assad the Younger

Bashar's inaugural speech on 17 July 2000 signalled a radical departure from the posture adopted by his father. The new President Assad presented himself as the reformer president. His carefully formulated address developed the concept that political power demands a sense of responsibility not only on the part of the political figure invested with it, but ideally in the citizenry as a whole. 'The ideal state of affairs,' he said, 'is that everyone should feel responsible and this does not mean that everyone should occupy a post.'[22] All must participate in some form: 'Thus society will not develop, improve or prosper if it were to depend only on one sect or one party or one group; rather, it has to depend on the work of all citizens in the entire society. That is why I find it absolutely necessary to call upon every single citizen to participate in the process of development and modernization if we are truly honest and serious in attaining the desired results in the very near future.'

Concretely, he proposed the renewal and improvement of old ideas or their replacement; he solicited 'constructive criticism' and urged citizens to develop 'objective opinion', considering both the negative and the positive of issues or policies. He went on to state: 'Today we need economic, social and scientific strategies that may serve both development and steadfastness' and this requires 'time, effort, cooperation as well as extensive and broad dialogues'. To elaborate such strategies, one must have accurate data and 'transparency', understood as 'a state of culture, values and social habits'.

Through his bold presentation, Bashar stressed cooperation among citizens and state institutions as a dynamic process: 'You should not rely solely on the State nor should you let the State rely solely on you: let us work together as one team.' The tasks he laid out included economic improvement through modernization of laws and enhanced investment in the public and private sector. Agriculture, too, should be modernized. 'Administrative reform is a pressing need for all of us today,' he said, as is a 'clean and efficient' functioning of the judiciary. In addition, 'reform and improvement are certainly needed in our educational, cultural and information institutions in a way that serves our national interests and strengthens our general culture that leads in turn to undermine the mentality of isolationism and passivism and addresses the social phenomena that negatively affect the unity and safety of our society.' Bashar explicitly called for 'democratic thinking', to generate 'democratic practices', and qualified this 'democratic experience' as tailored to meet Syria's needs with respect to its history and culture. In the overall social enterprise, women have a key role to play.

The inauguration address was a landmark in Syrian history, and was music to the ears of those millions of citizens who, having grown up under the oppressive autocratic reign of Hafiz al-Assad, dreamed of a better tomorrow. He called for citizen participation in a national reform effort, and they heeded the call, ushering in what was to become known as the 'Damascus spring'.

Once in office, Bashar did make some changes. After only a few weeks, he replaced the editors-in-chief of the two official papers, *al-Thawra* and *Tishrin*, as well as the state press agency SANA. At the same time, he released the first batch of 600 political prisoners in October, to be followed by periodic amnesties, and announced that Mezzah prison, used for political prisoners, would be turned into a hospital. Bringing in a new layer of younger Syrians, mainly with academic and business backgrounds, he set up advisory teams in his first year, like the 'Group of 18', for example, who were to counsel him on economic matters.[23] By the end of the following year, the new president had replaced three-quarters of the officials in military, administrative and political posts.[24] Some military and intelligence personnel were removed because Bashar saw them as standing in the way of his plans. By early 2004, he integrated 14 technocrats, mainly PhDs who had studied in the West.[25] Appointees from academia also filled important diplomatic posts.

With this new team, and the apparent will to introduce freedom of the press, Bashar raised hopes in the population of real and substantial change. Leading intellectual, political and liberal layers welcomed his new message by spearheading a social dialogue process, through informal salons and in the pages of the briefly liberalized press. Civil society organizations like the Friends of Civil Society came into being, flanked by human rights organizations, like the Committees for the Defence of Democratic Freedoms and Civil Rights, and the Syrian Human Rights Committee. Emboldened by what they thought was a commitment on the part of the new president to usher in a democratization process, members of the civil society issued the Statement (or the Manifesto) of 99 on 27 September 2000, in which they called for greater freedoms. The text pressed for:

> an end to the State of Emergency and martial law in effect in Syria since 1963
>
> an amnesty for all political prisoners and prisoners of conscience and those who are pursued because of their political ideas and permission for the return of all deportees and exiled citizens
>
> the establishment of a state of law; the granting of political freedoms; the recognition of political and intellectual pluralism, freedom of assembly, the press and of expression
>
> the liberation of public life from the [restrictive] laws, constraints and [various] forms of censorship imposed on it, such that citizens would be allowed to express their various interests within a framework of social harmony, peaceful competition and an institutional structure that would enable all to participate in the country's development and prosperity ...'[26]

The Statement of 1,000 or Basic Document, issued in January 2001, went beyond these ideas, implicitly promoting the introduction of a multi-party system. In presenting their philosophical outlook, the signatories state that:

> social groups and political parties are defined by the entire national social entity.

In its list of required measures, the document contains the following:

> 4. Enactment of a democratic election law to regulate elections at all levels in a way that ensures all segments of society are represented fairly, and the electoral process should be subjected to the supervision of an independent judiciary. The parliament elected as a result of this process will be a genuine legislative supervisory institution, truly representing the will of the people, acting as the highest authoritative reference for all and symbolizing the people's membership in the country and their positive participation in deciding how it is governed.

In point 7, the document suggests phasing out the one-party system under the Progressive National Front: 'It is imperative to review the relationship of the PNF with the government, to reconsider the concept of "the leading party in society and the state", and to review any other concept that excludes the people from political life.'

The 1,000 also demand full economic rights and equal rights for women.[27]

Both documents represented well-formulated, intelligent and responsible blueprints for turning Bashar's rhetoric into reality. Significantly, the content and tone of the petitions indicate a desire to work *with* and *through* the government to achieve these steps towards democracy. Not long after the publication of the second petition, Bashar gave an interview that was interpreted as his drawing the red line regarding any activity on the part of civil society that might threaten national stability. As published on 8 February 2001 in *Asharq Al-Awsat*, he stated:

> When the consequences of an action affect the stability of the homeland, there are two possibilities … either the perpetrator is a foreign agent acting on behalf of an outside power, or else he is a simple person acting unintentionally. But in both cases a service is being done to the country's enemies and consequently both are dealt with in a similar fashion, irrespective of their intentions or motives.[28]

That Bashar was in fact issuing the death sentence to the Damascus spring, and the beginning of a new regime of vicious repression became clear in subsequent events. That very month, meetings of the various informal salons and discussion groups came to a halt. In spring, the new editor of *al-Thawra* was sacked, and *al-Dommari*, a popular satirical weekly that had just been licensed, came under pressure, leading to its eventual demise. Arrests of outspoken activists and parliamentarians who promoted multi-party politics followed. An official of the Ba'ath Party declared on 21 February that the signatories of such documents had 'misunderstood' Bashar's inaugural address and had crossed 'red lines'. In April, Defence Minister Mustafa Tlas appeared on Abu Dhabi television, stating that he had 'evidence' that the 1,000 signatories were US intelligence agents, a claim allegedly proven by the fact that the Arab–Israeli conflict was not mentioned in the document.[29] In September a new decree regulated publications, allowing licences but only to those the government approved, and on condition that nothing about 'national security, national unity, and details of secret trials' be printed. There was 'talk' of reviewing the emergency law, and 'talk' of allowing other parties into the PNF, but Bashar said in an interview on 3 May 2005 that he '[felt] it [was] too soon to do this by 2007, but he mentioned it [was] certainly a possibility after his second term'.[30]

Bashar himself did not like the use of the term 'Damascus spring'. As he put it:

> Using the reference to Prague spring is incorrect for two reasons: (1) the Prague spring was in large measure imported from the outside – we did not have that here; and (2) the Prague spring was a political movement against the government, while in Syria I *started* it as president. I did not give a speech regarding political openness to get elected – I gave it after I was elected. Stability is important … We are very cautious … We take small steps, and if we do it wrong, we take another step. So in some things we go back – we did not take the right way. But I do not use the word 'spring'.[31]

To be sure, other tumultuous events in the region influenced developments, like the September 2000 Intifada and the demise of the Oslo peace process, but clearly there was a political shift taking place inside Syria, which may or may not have reflected a power struggle between the old guard and the Bashar establishment which he was piecing together – the common explanation.

Bashar must have taken very small steps, and very few of them, for, after ten years in power, nothing had improved. *The Guardian*, in a retrospective analysis, recalled that the younger Assad's inaugural address had been welcomed as 'the end of a nightmare' and 'a breath of fresh air'. Then came the backlash, and only one year later. *The Guardian*, duly noting the ritual explanation that the 'old guard' held him back, raised the question of why he didn't act after having consolidated power with his own people. Referencing Bashar's repeated claim that economic reforms had to take precedence over democratization, *The Guardian* pointed out that the repressive wave had, however, begun as early as August 2001. The article ended by quoting one dissident who characterized the change under Bashar in the following terms: 'In the 1980s, we went to jail without trial. Now, we get a trial, but we still go to jail.'[32]

An Antisocial Regime

In sum, it appears to have been a carefully crafted deception game, from the fairy tale accounts of the non-succession to the failure of reform due to 'old guard' resistance. (The deception game apparently did not begin with Bashar, but with his father. When Hafiz let it be known that he had suffered a heart attack in 1983, some Syrians reported that it was a ruse. The wily old man wanted to test his rivals and see who might challenge his power in the event that news of his falling seriously ill were broadcast. His brother Rifa'at did just that, attempting a coup, and was roundly defeated.)

Anyone who, after 11 years of empty promises under conditions of continuing police state rule, still lent credibility to the reformist posture of Bashar had to abandon all illusions once the protests broke out in March 2011 and the authorities responded with unexpected cruelty. For, at the same time that Bashar issued a decree abolishing the hated emergency law, his security units were shooting citizens in the streets. A new, not yet drafted law on public assembly was allegedly in force, whereby only demonstrations authorized by the interior ministry would be allowed. The notion was that, since the old emergency law had been dumped, there would no longer be any reason for Syrians to take to the streets.

As indicated earlier, for such a long-term deception operation to work the main protagonist had to possess the psychological capability to act out his role according to the script. The question then is: what kind of psychological makeup lends itself to such a deception operation? According to clinical studies by psychoanalysts in this field, the type under consideration is characterized by an *antisocial personality disorder*. This type of person stands out for the fact that he does *not* overtly manifest any recognizable signs of neurotic, let alone psychotic behaviour. He is intelligent, sometimes with a very high IQ, totally at ease in social situations, likeable and from every standpoint 'normal'. He can discuss problems logically and rationally, even accept criticism and engage in self-criticism.

But – and here lies the clue to the problem – he is insincere, misrepresenting in the most convincing manner. 'Typically, he is at ease and unpretentious in making a serious promise or in (falsely) exculpating himself from accusations, whether grave or trivial', the clinical psychiatrist tells us. Such a personality 'denies emphatically all responsibility and directly accuses others as responsible' and he appears to be blameless. This was the case in Bashar's ABC appearance, when he denied being in command and expressed no sense of shame or guilt. And, 'instead of facing facts that would ordinarily lead to insight, he projects, blaming his troubles on others with the flimsiest of pretext but with elaborate and subtle rationalization'.[33]

This clinical profile seems to fit Bashar like a tailor-made suit. As presented in detail in his official biography, Bashar projects the image of a modest, unassuming, unpretentious, rational, intelligent, well-educated person, who is even capable of self-criticism. Yet, he is not very sincere. His portrayal of his rise to power after Basil's death – i.e. in the succession myth – does not hold up under close examination of the facts. His ability to present situations in a false light is most notable in his relatively rare, but extremely revealing, interviews in the international press, like *The Wall Street Journal* piece or his appearance on the Charlie Rose show in May 2010, or his PR campaign with *The Telegraph*, *The Sunday Times* and ABC in late 2011.[34] When his assertions are weighed against reality, it becomes undeniable that he is not speaking the truth – all the while looking his interviewer directly in the face and sporting a slight, shy smile. In all his public addresses during the crisis, as well as in his *tête-à-tête* with the British and American press, Bashar displayed this clinical behaviour, denouncing conspiracies and pledging reforms while his police and military were firing on unarmed civilians.

When confronted with the failure of policies and actions which have caused distress to others, this personality type 'seems to have little or no ability to feel the significance of his situation, to experience the real emotions of regret or shame or determination to improve, or to realize that this is lacking. His clever statements have been hardly more than verbal reflexes; even his facial expressions are without the underlying content they imply.'[35] This is a fitting description of Bashar's demeanour during some of his speeches and interviews. Whether laughing hysterically at his own antics, as he did in Parliament, or outlining his ambitious programme for democratization to students at Damascus University with a deadpan expression or telling Barbara Walters he had given no orders, his outward attitude bore little correspondence to his words.

Related to this is the characteristic lack of empathy. After his security units had begun to open fire with live ammunition on peaceful citizens, Bashar seemed to show no sense of regret or remorse, and only in his second and third speeches did he pay lip service to respect for the 'martyrs' (on all sides).

Bashar's apparent inability to display normal emotions in tragic circumstances has a documented history; when his brother died, 'he tried not to be emotional, as is his demeanor', and after his father died, '[h]e really did not have time to be emotional.'[36] Photographs of Bashar at his father's funeral and at a commemoration ceremony a year later tend to reinforce this impression.[37] And, as he himself stressed in his *Times* interview, he is not wont to react emotionally.

Regarding the Syrian president's failure to introduce the reforms he had promised back in 2000, the scientific literature on the phenomenon notes that '[d]espite his excellent rational powers', this personality type 'continues to show the most execrable judgment about attaining what one might presume to be his ends'.[38] Thus, even if one entertains the hypothesis that Bashar were at some level 'sincere' about his reform agenda, he certainly proved to be constitutionally incapable of achieving his aims.

Here one must interpolate the factor of the real and presumed political and institutional obstacles to reform. The constant refrain one has heard not only from Assad apologists but also would-be objective analysts is that Bashar would have liked to reform Syrian society but could not because political power lay in the hands of a small elite of interlocking political/economic/military/intelligence interests, including the Alawite minority and the Assad/Makhlouf family networks. There is something to this reading. According to numerous reports issued on the occasion of the 2011 crisis, Syria had been ruled as Communist East Germany had been: there the state had several all-powerful security agencies which had recruited informers from all levels of society, such that there was at least one 'informal collaborator' (as they were called) known to be living in every apartment house, or working in every office or teaching in every school. According to one account, Syrian security organizations employed 65,000 people full time and hundreds of thousands part time. This means that there was one agent for every 257 overall population, or one agent for every 153 adults in Syrian society.[39] In addition, Syria's intelligence agencies also kept tabs on each other, to prevent any one body from attempting a power move. It was the security apparatus as a whole, with its various Mukhabarat departments, that ran the country and stood above the party in terms of power.

That the president is formally speaking as the supreme head does not mean that he actually makes all decisions. In this sense perhaps there is ironically a grain of truth in Bashar's argument on ABC that he was 'only' the president and did not 'own' the country. As several commentators noted during the uprising, Bashar was put into a seemingly inextricable bind: if he made concessions to the protesters, not only would they demand more – including his replacement – but other, hardline factions in his regime would balk, even to the point perhaps of pulling a coup against him.[40]

Because of the features of his personality, Bashar has been described as 'weak', and powerful figures in the hierarchy, above all his sister Bushra, her husband Assef Shaukat and his brother Lieutenant Colonel Maher al-Assad, Head of the Presidential Guard, as well as other security chiefs, had reportedly 'taken advantage' of this weakness.

In this complex situation it is therefore difficult to speak of a president who, due to a personality disorder, acts in this way or that. Rather, taking into account the history and pre-history of the Bashar phenomenon, it is more appropriate to speak of a *regime* which displays such an antisocial personality disorder: Bashar provides the cover, so to speak, the friendly face of reformer, while the agencies actually wielding power exert the brute force associated with this psychological phenomenon. The psychological syndrome is not embodied in one person; rather it is a system erected with Bashar's accession to power, a system which maintained and perfected the means of social control developed by Hafiz, but with a dramatically different outward appearance in the person of Bashar.

One way in which Bashar could have saved the situation and his own fate would have been to deploy his power base and mobilize his immense popular support – when he still had it – to find the ways and means of overcoming, outflanking or even eliminating the competing political interests of a tiny elite. As late as mid-December, Jürgen Todenhöfer, a German journalist and former political figure, shared his assessment from Syria that Bashar could at that point still solve the crisis politically. To do so, Todenhöfer proposed, he must call presidential elections, even at the risk of losing; separate himself from the existing regime; pull the tanks out of urban centres, and open a dialogue with the opposition, including the armed rebels. Once the crisis had degenerated into civil war, and death estimates reached 40,000 in late 2012, the opportunity for such a move had vanished.

If Yemeni leader Abdullah Saleh reminds us of King Lear, Bashar al-Assad may recall a tragic figure in Friedrich Schiller's drama *Don*

Carlos. There we see a young freedom-fighter, Marquis de Posa, who appeals to the king to break out of his historical stereotype and recognize the aspirations of his people to freedom. 'Be of a million kings the king', he pleads; 'Give them in Flanders, the freedom of thought'. But King Philip is incapable, both psychologically and institutionally. In place of bold political action, the court players engage in intrigue and plots. Had Bashar al-Assad responded differently to the initial requests for reform, he would have become an inspiration for the Arab world and beyond, instead of presiding over a tragedy of yet to be measured proportions.

NOTES
—

1 For an in-depth, informed presentation of the complexities of the Syrian crisis, see Harling, Peter and Sarah Birke, 'Beyond the Fall of the Syrian Regime', *MERIP*, 24 February 2012, http://www.merip.org/mero/mero022412. On the opposition: Skelton, Charlie, 'The Syrian Opposition: Who's Doing The Talking?', http://www.guardian.co.uk/commentisfree/2012/jul/12/syrian-opposition-doing-the-talking; Abukhalil, As'ad, 'Syria: Against the Syrian National Council', 8 March 2012, http://www.jadaliyya.com/pages/index/4593/opposition-to-the-syrian-opposition_against-the-sy; Landis, Joshua, 'Upheaval within the Opposition: Defections, Terrorism, and Preparing for a Phase II Insurgency', Syria Comment Blog, 19 March 2012; Hauben, Ronda, 'The United Nations and the Houla Massacre: The Information Battlefield', *Global Research*, 12 June 2012; Ramadani, Sami and Samuel Grove, 'Between Imperialism and Repression', *New Left Project*, 12 June 2012; Rosenthal, John, 'German Intelligence: al-Qaeda all over Syria', *Asia Times*, 24 July 2012; Dick, Martin, 'Islamist rebels challenge National Coalition', *The Daily Star*, 21 November 2012. For one among many strategic blueprints for manipulating the crisis, see Byman, Daniel and Michael Doran, Kenneth Pollack, and Salman Shaikh, 'Saving Syria: Assessing Options for Regime Change', *Middle East Memo*, Saban Center at Brookings, March 2012.

2 Lesch, David W., *The New Lion of Damascus: Bashar al-Asad and Modern Syria*, Yale University Press, New Haven and London, 2005, p. 230.

3 Ibid., p. 59.

4 Ibid., pp. 60–62.

5 Darraj, Susan Muaddi, *Bashar al-Assad*, Chelsea House, Philadelphia, 2005, p. 77.

6 AlJazeera, 25 March 2011 profile, Leverett, Flynt, *Inheriting Syria: Bashar's Trial by Fire*, Brookings Institution Press, Washington, DC, 2005, pp. 61, 64.

7 Darraj, op. cit., p. 78.

8 Leverett, ibid., p. 67.

9 Ibid., p. 62.

10 Ibid., p. 63, Lesch, op. cit., p. 67, van Dam, Nikolaos, *The Struggle for Power in Syria: Power and Politics under Asad and the Ba'th Party*, I. B. Tauris, London, 2011, p. 132.

11 Lesch, ibid., pp. 63–64. See 'Bashar al-Assad's inner circle', BBC NEWS Middle East, bbc.co.uk, 18 May 2011 for a detailed account of his network.

12   Ibid., p. 64.
13   Ibid., p. 75.
14   *TIME*, 13 November 1992, quoted by van Dam, op. cit., p. 132.
15   Lesch, op. cit., p. 67. Bashar himself however provided a tell-tale hint that he knew well in advance about succession plans. According to Foreign Minister Farouk Al-Sharaa speaking to the Lebanese paper *al-Mustaqbal* on 10 April 2000, two months prior to the death of Hafiz: 'Staff Colonel Bashar al-Asad told me more than once that President Asad does not intend to bequeath me a dishonourable peace and that he himself does not accept it either.' Ziadeh, Radwan, *Power and Policy in Syria: The Intelligence Services, Foreign Relations and Democracy in the Modern Middle East*, I. B. Tauris, London, 2011, p. 46.
16   Leverett, op. cit., p. 24.
17   Perthes, Volker, *Syria under Bashar al-Asad: Modernisation and the Limits of Change*, Adelphi Paper, The International Institute for Strategic Studies, Oxford University Press, Oxford, July 2004, p. 12.
18   Leverett, op. cit., pp. 25–26. 'He founded institutional structures to provide the democratic façade behind which he could exercise the real power of his party', Ziadeh, op. cit., p. 19.
19   Zahler, Kathy A., *The Assads' Syria*, Twenty-First Century Books, Minneapolis, 2010, p. 71.
20   Ibid., p. 168.
21   Lesch, op. cit., pp. 16, 12.
22   The full text of the speech can be found at http://www.al-bab.com/arab/countries/syria/bashar00a.htm.
23   Leverett, op. cit., pp. 168–169, 73.
24   Perthes, op. cit., p. 9.
25   Leverett, op. cit., pp. 78, 82.
26   Full text of document reproduced in Leverett, ibid., p. 204.
27   Ibid., pp. 207–212. See Perthes, op. cit., pp. 29–31 on the urgent need for economic reforms: 40 per cent of the population in 2004 was under the age of 15, 52 per cent were under the age of 20, and overall 20 per cent of the population were jobless. The top 5 per cent 'are estimated to control 50 per cent of national income', while '10 per cent of Syria's children between ten and 16 years of age are working for pay'.
28   Lesch, op. cit., p. 92.
29   Leverett, op. cit., pp. 94, 172–173.
30   Lesch, op. cit., pp. 94, 227.
31   Ibid., p. 90. Bashar displayed great sensitivity to certain words, for example, 'reform', and preferred to refer to 'development', Ziadeh, op. cit., p. 51.
32   *The Guardian*, 'Syria's Decade of Repression', by Nadim Houry, Guardian.co.uk, 16 July 2010.
33   Cleckley, Hervey, M.D., op. cit., pp. 387, 389, 400.
34   Charlie Rose, http://tv.yahoo.com/charlie-rose/show/29522/videos.
35   Cleckley, op. cit., p. 401.
36   Lesch, op. cit., pp. 3, 77.
37   Ibid., p. 66 and cover photo.
38   Cleckley, op. cit., p. 393.
39   Ziadeh, op. cit., pp. 23–24.
40   Hermann, Rainer, 'Divide, Conquer, Kill', *Frankfurter Allgemeine Zeitung (FAZ)*, 27 April 2011.

7

Postscript: The American Narcissus

The Arabs are not the only people who have suffered under the yoke of leaders afflicted by psychological disorders like narcissism and paranoia. There have been cases of profoundly psychologically disturbed persons in positions of power in Europe, most recently in nations formerly part of the Soviet bloc or sphere of influence – Slobodan Milošević being a case in point. But even in the 'free world', such figures have gained power and abused that power to inflict suffering on their own people and others. The Arabs have also been victims of such leaders from outside the Arab world, as they suffered the consequences of the severe psychological problems of a man who became US president and even won re-election: George W. Bush.

Prior to his entering the White House in 2001, as governor of Texas, Bush had already displayed manifold symptoms of narcissism, in particular, extreme brutality in his readiness to send prisoners to the electric chair and refuse pardons or stays of execution. He reportedly also attended executions and appeared to enjoy the killings with sadistic pleasure, as shown by the grin on his face. He continued to show a general lack of empathy as encountered in narcissists and sociopaths later when, as president, he was to send soldiers into war in Iraq and Afghanistan. No statistical reports of the cruel civilian casualties, including graphic depictions of suffering among children in Iraq, could move him emotionally and, convinced that he had a mandate from God, he continued his holy war of Good against Evil. The only regret Bush publicly acknowledged was that the intelligence regarding Saddam Hussein's weapons of mass destruction had been inaccurate. But he maintained that ridding Iraq and the world of Saddam Hussein had been worth all the suffering and destruction.

Like the cases of narcissism examined in the Arab revolution, Bush too experienced trauma as a child. As described in the seminal psychological profile by Dr Justin Frank, 'George W. was six years old at the beginning of the tragic episode that he has said yielded his first vivid childhood memories – the illness and death of his sister.' His parents took the child, diagnosed with leukaemia, to special clinics for treatment, but in vain. 'Critically, however,' writes Dr Frank, 'young George W. was never informed of the reason for the sudden absences; unaware that his sister was ill, he was simply told not to play with the girl, to whom he had grown quite close, on her occasional visits home.' When she died in 1953 in New York, his parents spent time playing golf, then participated in a small memorial ceremony. Incredibly Bush 'learned of his sister's illness only after the death, when his parents returned to Texas, where the family remained while the child's body was buried in a Connecticut family plot. There was no funeral.' The lack of mourning had a devastating effect.[1]

Bush also had serious reading and learning problems as a child, with symptoms of Attention Deficit Disorder that continued into adulthood, whence his famous difficulties in articulating comprehensible sentences. He suffered from a deep inferiority complex, especially with regard to his father, a well-known public figure, as well as his brother, and put himself psychologically in competition with them. He expressed sadism at an early age, delighting in torturing small animals like frogs.

His sister's death, which he acknowledged as the most important event in his life, generated a deep-rooted fear in the child and, in Dr Frank's analysis, Bush developed into a narcissist with extreme paranoia, as a means to manage his anxiety. Alcoholism became another tool and, after his being 'born again' as a fundamentalist Christian, religion served as another crutch – all to attempt to ward off or control anxiety. Cheap humour, which he referred to as 'clowning', was also a trick he could use to defend himself from perceived threats, during interviews for example. To ensure he would not be put on the spot in public, he deployed his security personnel to carefully screen attendants at any event. Any direct challenge to his authority, Frank explains, could throw him into a crisis.

This happened during his first televised debate in 2004 when John Kerry challenged Bush's competence by saying that he had made mistakes his father would never have made. Given the competitive relationship he had with Bush Sr., George W. 'became … completely unwound and unraveled', as Dr Frank put it in an interview. His only response was, 'Of course, I know the difference between Saddam Hussein and Bin Laden', a disconnected statement which revealed his state of anxiety and fear of humiliation. Another example Dr Frank cites of Bush's inability to think, especially when under pressure, was his reaction to a journalist's impromptu question, 'How come we haven't caught Bin Laden?' The answer was, 'Because he's hiding!'

Like other political figures afflicted by this disorder, Bush divided the world and its people into black and white categories of Good and Evil. Especially in the aftermath of the terrorist attacks on 11 September 2001, he took it as a personal mission to defeat Evil – i.e. terrorism – and every citizen had to take sides, to be either 'with me or against me.' In Dr Frank's analysis, Bush's obsession with pursuing 'freedom', was actually a projection: that is, 'What he wants is freedom from anxiety.'[2] The religious conversion he underwent while giving up alcohol led Bush to believe that he was receiving instructions from God. He reported that God had told him to fight Al Qaida, and so he did, then God told him to fight Saddam Hussein, and so he did. Enjoying authority from such high places, Bush felt he was above the law and could therefore violate international conventions on torture and war crimes, as well as tear up the US Constitution and issue Executive Orders in its place.

Though not comparable in form with the authoritarian regimes in Libya, Egypt or Syria, the United States under two terms of Bush in office saw an unprecedented restriction in civil liberties, including personal surveillance procedures that were reminiscent of police states. Again the justification for such measures was the fight against terrorism.

Ms America, Sarah Palin

The constituency that allowed Bush to win the elections was predominantly Christian fundamentalist, estimated to represent almost the majority of the voter base in the Republican Party. His appeal to this sector of the population, also known as Christian Zionists because of their strict interpretation of the Old Testament, was grounded in his purportedly deep religiosity, and his commitment to a holy crusade against the 'axis of Evil' and related terrorists. Since the 2008 elections, this social base has forged a new movement, known as the Tea Party, largely rooted in the Republican Party, and has found a new voice in the person of Sarah Palin.

Ms Palin, who was John McCain's running mate in the 2008 elections, has emerged as a national figure with all the landmarks of the narcissistic personality disorders reviewed thus far. But hers has a distinctly American cultural flavour. Palin's grandiose self is not exhibited in monumental statues or posters in public places, but in the image of her continuing struggle to dominate savage nature. In her reality show, a television series on prime time Sunday nights entitled *Palin's Alaska*, Sarah would appear with her family in various confrontations with the powers of nature. For instance, one episode showed her with her husband Todd scaling a glacier on Mt McKinley. Equipped with ropes and prodded by a guide who is above her, she struggles to place one foot after the other on the rock, but fails to get a foothold and shouts a desperate plea, 'Oh God. Help me, Lord!' followed by 'I'm scared … Holy Jeez!' While television viewers, chewing on potato chips and sipping beer, gasp in awe, Sarah continues her climb and much later succeeds in reaching the top. Her victory is the victory of sheer will power, and expresses her conviction that, if the effort expended is great enough, one can overcome any obstacle. This is the credo of self-reliance of the free individual.

In another episode, Sarah takes her daughter Bristol on a fishing expedition in Homer, Alaska, the capital of halibut fishing. Her daughter, who had an illegitimate child and a broken marriage, had been the target of the 'liberal press', one of Palin's favourite enemy images. So Sarah thought she would teach her daughter how to become self-reliant. First they go to a shooting range to practise skeet-shooting. Although Bristol has never shot a gun, her mother convinces her that she can do it if she perseveres. Each time that Bristol aims, shoots and misses the target, her mother repeats, 'Don't retreat, reload.' Bristol follows her orders and after trying again and yet again, she finally hits the clay pigeon in mid-air, whereupon general jubilation follows.

'Don't retreat, reload!' it turns out, was the instruction Sarah's father had issued to her as a child, when she learned to handle weapons. 'She started shooting a gun when she was eight,' he told *The Sun* in an interview, 'and shot her first animal when she was ten. It was something small, possibly a rabbit,' he added. But it would not be long before she took on bigger game. 'She really is a good shot,' he went on, 'I taught her to shoot a moose and dress it, to fish and hunt for game.' The ideology behind this is again self-reliance, an ideology embraced by entire communities in the United States who, living in rural retreats, depend only on their own hands to bring in food to survive.

To return to the episode with Bristol: having succeeded in shooting a clay pigeon, her daughter accompanies her on a boat to cast nets for halibut. When, after several unsuccessful attempts, again Bristol finally nabs a fish, she has to pull it up onto the deck and heave it down into a hold full of ice. There, she has to wield what looks like a huge baseball bat to 'stun' the fish, knock it unconscious, so it can later be slaughtered. She must then take knife in hand and, following her mother's example, butcher the bloody fish.

According to the professional literature, narcissistic enhancement, or gratification from such an achievement, comes only when the individual has succeeded in the endeavour through sheer will power. 'Successes in imposing one's own will are enjoyed by a being with self-consciousness not only because of their consequences, but also as ends in themselves,' writes Vittorio Hösle. 'Thus a man [or a woman] experiences the magnitude of the opposition that he has overcome – in the case of hunting, for instance, in relation to the dangerousness of the animal killed.'[3] Sarah, as noted by her father, was good at shooting moose even as a child. And moose can be *very* dangerous.

Her parents, as she writes in her book, *America by Heart*, brought up the children to learn through experience the 'pioneering work ethic' and self-reliance typical of the part of America where she grew up, Alaska. So Sarah learned to hunt, fish, chop wood for heating and grow vegetables. She was also on hand when her daughter gave birth, and performed the services of a midwife. Palin has presented her grandiose self as a role model for today's generation of female leaders in America, whom she calls 'Mama Grizzlies'. A mama grizzly is a female grizzly bear that has to protect her offspring; as anyone familiar with wildlife knows, such bears are extremely dangerous, especially when they fear that their young may be threatened. Therefore, one should approach with caution, because they can attack. This type of woman, she explains, is actually not new but has always been a part of American culture. During the conquest of the frontier, for example, such women worked on the farm and not only brought up their children but took care of livestock too. Finally, they were also politically active.[4]

It was Palin's need for attention and approval that led her to enter politics. Although a neophyte when she ran in 2008, with no foreign policy experience not to mention knowledge, she plunged confidently onto the public arena. In what is typical of American political culture, she cheerfully combined her ignorance with arrogance, and made a bid as someone capable of leading America and the free world. In an interview with Charles Gibson on ABC during the campaign, she warned, 'We have to keep our eyes on Russia. Under the leadership there.' And she stressed the unique vantage point she had, living in Juneau, Alaska, to do this, since 'You can actually see Russia from here.' So, 'We have to keep our eyes on Russia.'

Palin stressed that the US must be 'wired into the mission', i.e. the mission of winning the war on terrorism and any other wars that may have to be fought. One possible conflict she referenced was with Russia; if Georgia were to join NATO, as she and McCain proposed, and if Russia attacked Georgia, then the US should militarily intervene. Nor does she shun war against Iran.

Like Bush, Palin is a Christian fundamentalist, a member of the Wasilla Assembly of God from the age of ten, and rebaptised there two years later. When she became governor of Alaska, she began attending the Juneau Christian Church, associated with something called the Third Wave Movement, whose belief structure includes the conviction that when the End Times come, then a group of Christians, influenced by supernatural powers, will take over the church and the world. For Palin, Alaska has also been given a divine mission: 'God has a destiny for the state of Alaska,' she announced in a video entitled 'Transformations', and that is to become the last refuge for all Americans when the End Times come.[5]

Her narcissism has a specifically American cultural flavour. In a sort of psychological projection of her grandiose self onto the world as a whole, she worships the notion of 'American exceptionalism', the idea that America is something unique in the world, and therefore better than any other nation – although she specifically denies it is 'better;' rather, it is a 'model' for all other nations. Palin did not invent the concept or the name, but she has organized a political movement around it, and a personality cult around her person as the movement's leader. Speaking of the Iraq war, in which her son fought, she ponders the differences between her nation and the other nations in the world. America, she writes, shares with all others the right to self-defense, but it distinguishes itself from the rest by virtue of its unique history. For it was neither land, nor language nor ethnicity that defined the foundation of America's identity when it was born as a nation; it was rather a concept: that all men are created equal.[6]

Palin refers to Puritan leader John Winthrop in 1620, when he spoke of America to his followers as the 'light of the world' and a 'city on a hill', phrases attributed to Christ in the Gospel of St Matthew. For Palin, America is a power of virtue for all of mankind, not only for its own citizens. Other characteristics she attributes to American exceptionalism are commitment to the free-market ideology, creativity and the work ethic.[7]

If America is special in the world, Alaska is special in America, and she is special in Alaska. In her book she writes of thoughts that occurred to her one day at the age of 11, when she was admiring the magnificent landscape and mountains. It is essentially an account of her religious experience as a born-again Christian. She marveled at two vast mountain ranges on either side, and was struck by the notion that if the Creator had a clear idea of His achievement when He brought such an awesome landscape into being, then there must have been a similar intention when He created a comparatively tiny being such as herself. She realized there must be a reason for her existence and, as if reborn, entrusted her life to God.[8]

This divine calling is what makes American exceptionalism so special for Palin. It essentially explains why Americans, unlike citizens of other nations (in her view), look to God for inspiration. The United States is also different from the Soviet Union which was atheist, and different from Europe, with its belief in the 'divine right of kings' and so on. American exceptionalism rests instead on the principle of what might be termed the divine right to freedom, and that, in turn, defines America's extraordinary global function.[9]

Like narcissistic personalities encountered in the Arab world, for example Leila Ben Ali Trabelsi, Palin is an ambitious, power-hungry woman, seeking monetary wealth as well as public admiration and fame. She left her post as Governor of Alaska in a move that seemed in the state to have little political justification, and sought a prominent role in national politics as the Tea Party standard bearer. Appearing regularly as a political commentator on Fox TV, the television outlet of the radical right wing in America, as well as launching her own reality show, she built up a mass following, which also ensured that her books would be commercial successes. With both books, Palin travelled across the nation on speaking tours, promoting the publications and expanding her support among adulating crowds, especially of women, who would wait in line for hours to have a book autographed. Through such activity, she also made a lot of money – money she would need to finance her famously expensive wardrobes.

Sarah Palin, supported by experienced and capable public relations professionals, has also very consciously cultivated her image to resonate with certain precedents in the US political experience. In her 2008 campaign, she made a mark on the public with her image of the good old-fashioned, all-American girl, 'as American as apple pie'; she was the girl who avoids using rough language, preferring 'gosh' and 'darn' to their more extreme counterparts, the wholesome pretty girl from a typical American family and so on. For Americans old enough to remember, she evoked the memory of Debbie Reynolds, a famous movie star in the 1950s, who projected the image of the all-American girl.[10] Palin, like Reynolds, had also qualified in beauty contests and she copied Reynolds in her posture as well as hairstyle. It was not just this 'look' that counts. Most important to consider is that the 1950s was also the period of the Cold War, when popular culture, from movies to televisions series, propagated the image of good, clean Americans fighting to uphold the principles of freedom against the evil Communists, who were not only ruling the Soviet Union and China, but threatening to infiltrate the United States, as the McCarthy trials documented. Then, as now, the world was divided into Good and Evil. If the conflict then was perceived as between freedom and communism, for Palin it is between freedom and 'socialism' (her term for American liberal philosophy); states' rights and big government; proud patriotic Americans and East Coast liberals; Fox News and the leftist press, etc.

Sarah Palin made her bid for political power and was voted down, but she has not given up her ambitious dream of attaining national leadership, wealth and power. The fact that the American people elected such a labile, obviously disturbed personality as George W. and even accepted his second term speaks volumes about the unhealthy side of American political culture. It is not merely a matter of narcissism in these individuals, but also in the popular culture. In the run-up to the 2012 presidential campaign, almost all the candidates vying for the nomination on the Republican side exhibited textbook signs of narcissism. As one American analyst put it speaking of the Tea Party: 'The new Jacobins have two classic American traits that have grown much more pronounced in recent decades: blanket distrust of institutions and an astonishing

– and unwarranted – confidence in the self'; one might say, in the grandiose self.[11]

NOTES

1   Frank, Justin A., M.D., op. cit., p. 3. Dr Frank explained the psychological impact of his sister's death and particularly how the family dealt with it. '[I]t has to do with the fact that he was never able to mourn, and when you don't mourn, you can't integrate your inner life … Sorrow is the vitamin of growth, and until you face who you are and what you've lost, you really can't organize your mind, and so what happens is when you're the first born, and the next one dies, you're left with a lot of unworked-out hostility, anger, guilt, that maybe your wishes killed them.' *EIR*, 20 August 2004.

2   *EIR*, 4 February 2005

3   Hösle, V., *Morals and Politics*, Notre Dame: University of Notre Dame Press, 2004, cited in Wirth, Hans-Jürgen, op. cit., p. 73.

4   Palin, Sarah, *America by Heart: Reflections on Family, Faith, and Flag*, HarperCollins Publishers, New York, 2010, pp. 96, 127–128, 144, 128–129. Her first book was *Going Rogue: An American Life*, HarperCollins Publishers, New York, 2009. Palin's cult of self-reliance, her worship of American exceptionalism and her challenging the powers of nature recall the ideology of Italian fascist – and narcissist – Benito Mussolini in the 1920s and 1930s. For Mussolini, it was autarky, 'Italianità' and machismo, concepts embedded in a different cultural context but strikingly similar.

5   Mirak-Weissbach, Muriel, 'The Republicans' Subliminal Ticket: Will American Voters be Hoodwinked?' *Global Research*, 17 September 2008.

6   Palin, op. cit., p. 37.

7   Ibid., pp. 64, 67, 80.

8   Ibid., pp. 181–182

9   Ibid., pp. 190, 212, 223, 265.

10 Mirak-Weissbach, op. cit.

11 Lilla, Mark, 'The Tea Party Jacobins', in *The New York Review of Books*, 27 May to 9 June, 2010, p. 54.

8

The Good Ruler

Modern psychoanalytical methodology is of enormous help in understanding the dynamics of psychosis in leadership. There are, unfortunately, very few psychoanalysts and psychologists who have addressed the positive alternative issue: what makes for healthy political leadership? How can society organize itself in such a way as to generate moral, competent rulers, who are dedicated to the promotion of the common good?

Happily, there are some exceptions. One is Otto F. Kernberg, who defined five significant and desirable personality characteristics required for a rational leadership. They are: (1) intelligence; (2) personal honesty and incorruptibility; (3) the ability to establish and maintain intensive interpersonal relations; (4) a healthy narcissism; and (5) a healthy, legitimate anticipatory paranoid attitude which signifies (constitutes) the opposite of naïveté.[1] In the view of Max Weber, a sociologist, a good politician must be someone who is passionately devoted to a cause. He posed the challenge to the political leader in these terms:

> For the problem is simply how can warm passion and a cool sense of proportion be forged together in one and the same soul? Politics is made with the head, not with other parts of the body or soul. And yet devotion to politics, if it is not to be frivolous intellectual play but rather genuinely human conduct, can be born and nourished from passion alone. However, that firm taming of the soul, which distinguishes the passionate politician and differentiates him from the 'sterilely excited' and mere political dilettante, is possible only through habituation to detachment in every sense of the word. The 'strength' of a political personality means, in the first place, the possession of these qualities of passion, responsibility, and proportion.[2]

The search for moral leadership in politics has a long, fascinating history. From ancient China to India, to classical Greece, and through the

Arab renaissance into Europe, philosophers and statesmen have debated this issue passionately and proposed viable solutions. Without entering into a detailed account of this philosophical/political debate, consider one seminal work in the Arabic literature on the subject: the brilliant study by Al-Fārābī, in his book, *Arâ' ahl al-madīna l-fāḍila* (*The Ideal State*). The following short excerpt is his depiction of the just ruler – what qualities of mind and body a man must possess in order to provide leadership to his people in the pursuit of justice and the common good. This represents the best of the true Arab heritage in political science theory. In the wake of the ongoing revolutions, it would be desirable to see the new political leadership emerging from the process to launch an Arab renaissance – a revival of the philosophy and political science of great intellectuals like Al-Fārābī.

The Qualities of the Leader in the Ideal State

This ruler is one over whom no other man rules. He is the Imām (Head), he is the first sovereign of the excellent city, he is the leader of the most excellent people, the head of the whole inhabited world. No man is qualified for this position unless he possesses twelve qualities which nature has endowed him with from birth.

(a) He must have sound, healthy limbs, whose power is such that that they can carry out what they must carry out and, when he wishes to perform an action with one of his limbs, he can do so with ease.

(b) He should by nature possess a good capacity for understanding and perceiving everything said to him, in such a manner that with his understanding he grasps what the speaker intends, as the matter in effect is.

(c) Then he must retain what he has understood, observed and heard, in short, everything that he has grasped. He should not forget anything.

(d) He must be reasonable and perspicacious; if he discerns something from the slightest indication, he must grasp the full meaning from this indication alone.

(e) He must be able to express himself; his tongue must articulate clearly and completely to make known everything he wants to say.

(f) He must be fond of learning and acquiring knowledge, and grasp things easily. In the course of acquiring new knowledge, he must never tire and exhaustion should never scathe him.

(g) He must never crave for food or drink or carnal pleasure; he must by nature detest gambling as well as the pleasures derived from it.

(h) He must love truth and truthful men and hate falsehoods and liars.

(i) He must be magnanimous and dedicated to noble-mindedness; by nature his soul must be elevated above all that defiles, yea, he must rise above all even to the loftiest degree.

(j) Dirham and dinar (wealth) and the other worldly pursuits should have no value for him.

(k) He must by nature love justice and the just, and hate oppression and injustice and those who practise them. He should practise justice towards his own as well as others[;] he must urge others to do this. He must provide indemnity to those who have suffered injustice and he must applaud everything that he finds good and beautiful. He must be just, allow himself to be guided, be neither stubborn nor obstinate if he is asked to render justice; but if he is asked to do something unjust or disgraceful, then he must refuse.

(l) He should be determined to do what he considers necessary, and daringly and bravely carry it out without fear or weak-mindedness.

It is difficult to find all these qualities united in one man, and, therefore, men endowed with this nature will be found one at a time only, and they appear only very seldom among men. Now, if one finds such a man in the ideal city who, after reaching maturity, possesses the first six conditions or five of the twelve aforementioned conditions – excluding the power of imagination – he will be the sovereign. If, however, one does not find such a man in any specific time, then one should take the laws and customs established by the first ruler and his like, and which are to be handed down further, and confirm them.

The second ruler in rank, who is to succeed the first, is one who from birth, during adolescence and in adulthood, fulfils the following six conditions: first, he must be wise, a philosopher; second, he must be knowledgeable and must know, keep in mind, respect, and duly enforce the laws and customs as well as the changes of the elders who ruled the city. Third, by the power of deduction, he must set down that for which his predecessors had no laws. In this, he must follow the aim of the first Imām. Fourth, he must have a good power of reflection and deduction to fathom what he must at all times discern, regarding both the current situation and possible events to come which were not yet known to his predecessors. He must then reflect and practise in order to recognize how he can justify the well-being of the State through what he has brought forth.

Fifth, he must always be right when he presents the laws of his predecessors as well as when he carries out what was created on their example.

Sixth, he must be in good health to be able to master the conduct of war. This means that he must master the art of war, both in serving and in leading.

If one does not find one man who fulfils all these conditions, but one finds two men, the first of whom is wise and the other of whom possesses the other qualities, then both will be leaders of this city. If these conditions however are found only dispersed among many, one quality by one man, another by the second man, and so forth up to the sixth man, and if they are all in agreement with one another, then they will constitute the excellent leader together. If there comes a time when wisdom does not constitute any part of this leadership but the other conditions exist, then the ideal city remains without a king, the city will be threatened with destruction and, in the case that no wise man is found who can be added to the government, then it will not be long before the city goes under.[3]

NOTES

1   Kernberg, Otto F., *Ideologie, Konflikt und Führung: Psychoanalyse von Gruppenprozessen und Persönlichkeitsstruktur*, op. cit., p. 63. Wirth (op. cit., pp. 196–197) presents Kernberg's criteria ('Sanctioned Social Violence', in *International Journal of Psychoanalysis* 84, 2003, pp. 683–698) as follows: '(1) High intelligence, enabling the leader to apply long-range strategic thinking to diagnosing, formulating, communicating and implementing the requirements of the task within its constraints; (2) sufficient emotional maturity and human depth to be able to assess the personality of others in selecting subordinate leaders and delegating appropriate authority to them; (3) a solid and deep moral integrity that protects the leader from the unavoidable temptations intimately linked to the exercise of power and from the corrupting pressures of the leader's entourage; (4) sufficiently strong narcissistic tendencies to be able to maintain self-esteem in the face of the unavoidable criticism and attacks of the followers, and to avoid depending upon the followers for fulfilments of excessive narcissistic needs; (5) sufficient paranoid features – in contrast to naïveté – to diagnose early the unavoidable ambivalent and hostile undercurrents in the organization that express the resentful, rebellious and envious aspects of the aggression directed toward leadership.'

2   Weber, Max, 'Politics as Vocation', Speech delivered in Germany, January 1919. http://www.ne.jp/asahi/moriyuki/abukuma/weber/lecture/politics_vocation. html, p. 25. Wirth, ibid., p. 97.

3   *Der Musterstaat von Al Fārābī aus dem Arabischen* übertragen von Dr Friedrich Dieterici, Professor an der Universität Berlin, E.J. Brill, Leiden, 1900, pp. 94–97.

Bibliography

Al Aswany, Alaa, *On the State of Egypt: What Made the Revolution Inevitable*, translation by Jonathan Wright, Vintage Books, Random House, New York, April 2011.

Al-Fārābī, *Der Musterstaat von Al Fārābī aus dem Arabischen* übertragen von Dr Friedrich Dieterici, Professor an der Universität Berlin (*The Ideal State by Al Fārābī* translation from the Arabic by Dr Friedrich Dieterici, Professor at the University of Berlin), E.J. Brill, Leiden, 1900.

Al-Fārābī, *Traité des opinions des habitants de la cité idéale*, translation by Tahani Sabri (*Treatise on the Views of the Citizens of the Ideal State*), Libraire Philosophique J. Vrin, Paris, 1990.

Al-Fārābī, *On the Perfect State*, translation by Richard Walzer, Oxford University Press, Oxford, 1985.

Amin, Galal, *Egypt in the Era of Hosni Mubarak 1981–2011*, The American University in Cairo Press, Cairo, New York, 2011.

Ayoub, Mahmoud Mustafa, *Islam and the Third Universal Theory: The Religious Thought of Ma'ammar al-Qadhdhafi*, KPI, London, 1987.

Beau, Nicolas, and Catherine Graciet, *La régente de Carthage: main basse sur la Tunisie* (*The Regent of Carthage: Assault on Tunisia*), Éditions La Découverte, Paris, 2009.

Ben Chrouda, Lotfi, in collaboration with Isabelle Soares Boumalala, *Dans l'ombre de la reine* (*In the Shadow of the Queen*), Éditions Michel Lafon, Neuilly-sur-Seine Cedex, 2011.

Ben Jelloun, Tahar, *Arabischer Frühling: Vom Wiedererlangen der arabischen Würde* (*Arab Spring: On Regaining Arab Dignity*), translation from the French by Christiane Kayser, Bloomsbury Verlag GmbH, Berlin, 2011.

Ben Hamida, Amor, *Chronik einer Revolution: Wie ein Gemüsehändler einen Präsidenten stürzt* (*Chronicle of a Revolution: How a Street Vendor Overthrows a President*), Books on Demand GmbH, Norderstedt, 2011.

Benslama, Fethi, *Soudain la révolution! De la Tunisie au monde arabe: la signification d'un soulèvement* (*Suddenly Revolution! From Tunisia to the Arab World: the Meaning of a Rebellion*), Éditions Denoël, Paris, 2011.

Blundy, David, and Andrew Lycett, *Qaddafi and the Libyan Revolution*, Little, Brown and Company, Boston, Toronto, 1987.

Bradley, John R., *Inside Egypt: The Land of the Pharaohs on the Brink of Revolution*, Palgrave Macmillan, New York, 2009.

Cleckley, Hervey, M.D., *The Mask of Sanity: An Attempt to Clarify Some Issues About the So-called Psychopathic Personality*, Literary Licensing, LLC, Whitefish, MT, 2011.

Darraj, Susan Muaddi, *Bashar al-Assad*, Chelsea House, Philadelphia, 2005.

Darraj, Susan Muaddi, *Hosni Mubarak*, Chelsea House, New York, 2007.

Dresch, Paul, *A History of Modern Yemen*, Cambridge University Press, Cambridge, 2000, 2002.

Elaasar, Aladdin, *The Last Pharaoh: Mubarak and the Uncertain Future of Egypt in the Volatile Mid East*, Beacon Press, Montana, 2009.

Erdle, Steffen, *Ben Ali's 'New Tunisia' (1987–2009): A Case Study of Authoritarian Modernization in the Arab World*, Klaus Schwarz Verlag, Berlin, 2010.

Ezrow, Natasha M., and Erica Frantz, *Dictators and Dictatorships: Understanding Authoritarian Regimes and Their Leaders*, The Continuum International Publishing Group, New York, 2011.

Frank, Justin A., M.D., *Bush on the Couch: Inside the Mind of the President*, ReganBooks, an imprint of HarperCollins Publishers, New York, 2004, 2005.

Freud, Sigmund, *Totem and Taboo, Resemblances Between the Psychic Lives of Savages and Neurotics*, Random House, New York, 1918.

Freud, Sigmund, *Gesammelte Werke*, Chronologisch geordnet, 10. und 13. Band (*Collected Works*, chronologically ordered, Volumes 10 and 13), Imago Publishing Co., Ltd., London, 1947, 1949.

Freud, Sigmund, and Josef Breuer, *Studies on Hysteria*, The Hearst Corporation, New York, 1966.

Gaddafi, Muammar, with Edmond Jouve, *My Vision: Conversations and Frank Exchanges of Views with Edmond Jouve*, translation into English by Angela Parfitt, John Blake, London, 2005.

Ghaemi, Nassir, *A First-Rate Madness: Uncovering the Links between Leadership and Mental Illness*, The Penguin Press, New York, 2011.

Hare, Robert D., *Psychopathy: Theory and Research*, John Wiley & Sons, Inc., New York, London, Sydney, Toronto, 1970.

Harling, Peter, and Sarah Birke, 'Beyond the Fall of the Syrian Regime', *MERIP*, 24 February 2012, http://www.merip.org/mero/mero 022412.

Heikal, Mohamed, *The Road to Ramadan*, William Collins Sons & Co. Ltd., London, 1975.

Heikal, Mohamed, *Autumn of Fury: The Assassination of Sadat*, Andre Deutsch Limited, London, 1983.

Husic, Sead, *Psychopathologie der Macht: Die Zerstörung Jugoslawiens im Spiegel der Biografien von Milošević, Tudjman und Izetbegović* (*Psychopathology of Power: The Destruction of Yugoslavia as Reflected in the Biographies of Milošević, Tudjman and Izetbegović*), Verlag Hans Schiler, Berlin, 2007.

Kernberg, Otto F., *Aggression in Personality Disorders and Perversions*, Yale University Press, New Haven and London, 1992.

Kernberg, Otto F., *Love Relations: Normality and Pathology*, Yale University Press, New Haven and London, 1995.

Kernberg, Otto F., Herausgeber, *Narzißtische Persönlichkeitsstörungen* (Ed. *Narcissistic Personality Disorders*), translation into German and revision by Bernhard Strauß, Schattauer, Stuttgart, New York, 1996.

Kernberg, Otto F., *Ideologie, Konflikt und Führung: Psychoanalyse von Gruppenprozessen und Persönlichkeitsstruktur*, J.G. Cotta'sche Buchhandlung Nachfolger GmbH, Stuttgart, 2000, translation by Elisabeth Vorspohl (*Ideology, Conflict, and Leadership in Groups and Organizations*, Yale University Press, New Haven, 1998).

Kernberg, Otto F., *Aggressivity, Narcissism, and Self-Destructiveness in the Psychotherapeutic Relationship: New Developments in the Psychopathology and Psychotherapy of Severe Personality Disorders*, Yale University Press, New Haven, 2004.

Kohut, Heinz, M.D., *The Analysis of the Self: A Systematic Approach to the Psychoanalytic Treatment of Narcissistic Personality Disorders*, International Universities Press, Inc., New York, 1971.

Kohut, Heinz, *Narzißmus: Eine Theorie der psychoanalytischen Behandlung narzißtischer Persönlichkeitsstörungen* (*Narcissism: A Theory of*

Psychoanalytical Treatment of Narcissistic Personality Disorders), Suhrkamp Verlag, 1973.

Längle, Alfried, 'Personality Disorders and Genesis of Trauma: Existential Analysis of Traumatized Personality Disorders,' in *Existenzanalyse* 22, 2005.

Lawson, Fred H., *Demystifying Syria*, London Middle East Institute at SOAS, London, 2009.

Lesch, David W., *The New Lion of Damascus: Bashar al-Asad and Modern Syria*, Yale University Press, New Haven and London, 2005.

Leverett, Flynt, *Inheriting Syria: Bashar's Trial by Fire*, Brookings Institution Press, Washington, DC, 2005.

Lohmann, Heiner, *Strukturen mythischen Denkens im Grünen Buch Mu'ammar al-Qaddafis: Eine kommunikationstheoretische Untersuchung zur Rationalität eines soziozentrischen Weltbildes im Islam mit einer Neuübersetezung des Grünen Buches im Anhang* (*Structures of Mythical Thinking in Muammar Qaddafi's Green Book: A Communications Theory Examination of the Rationality of a Sociocentric World View in Islam with a new Translation of the Green Book in the Appendix*), LIT Verlag Dr W. Hopf, Berlin, 2009.

Lüders, Michael, *Tage des Zorns: Die arabische Revolution verändert die Welt* (*Days of Rage: The Arab Revolution Changes the World*), Verlag C.H. Beck, München, 2011.

Marley, Ben, *Webster's Guide to World Governments: Syria, featuring President Bashar al-Assad and Prime Minister Muhammad Naji al-Otari*, Six Degrees Books, Laverne, TN, 2011.

Mattes, Hanspeter, *Qaddafi und die islamische Opposition in Libyan* (*Qaddafi and the Islamic Opposition in Libya*), Deutsches Orient-Institut, Hamburg, 1995.

Murphy, Emma C., *Economic and Political Change in Tunisia: From Bourghiba to Ben Ali*, Macmillan Press Ltd, London, 1999.

Nordhausen, Frank, Thomas Schmidt (Hg.), *Die Arabische Revolution: Demokratischer Aufbruch von Tunesien bis zum Golf* (Eds. *The Arab Revolution: Democratic Awakening from Tunisia to the Gulf*), Ch. Links Verlag, Berlin, October 2011.

Palin, Sarah, *Going Rogue: An American Life*, HarperCollins Publishers, New York, 2009.

Palin, Sarah, *America by Heart: Reflections on Family, Faith, and Flag*, HarperCollins Publishers, New York, 2010.

Perthes, Volker, *Syria under Bashar al-Asad: Modernisation and the Limits of Change*, Adelphi Paper, The International Institute for Strategic Studies, Oxford University Press, Oxford, July 2004.

Qaddafi, Muammar, *Escape to Hell and Other Stories*, Stanké, New York, 1998.

Riemann, Fritz, *Anxiety: Using Depth Psychology to Find a Balance in Your Life*, translation by Greta Dunn (*Grundformen der Angst: Eine tiefenpsychologische Studie*), Ernst Reinhardt Verlag, München, 2006, 2009.

Sachse, Rainer, *Histrionische und Narzißtische Persönlichkeitsstörungen* (*Histrionic and Narcissistic Personality Disorders*), Hogrefe Verlag für Psychologie, Göttingen, Bern, Toronto, Seattle, 2002.

Sadek, Hassan, *Gaddafi*, Heinrich Hugendubel Verlag, Kreuzlingen/München, 2005.

Sharp, Gene, *From Dictatorship to Democracy: A Conceptual Framework for Liberation*, The Albert Einstein Institution, Fourth US Edition, 2010.

Sicker, Martin, *The Making of A Pariah State: The Adventurist Politics of Muammar Qaddafi*, Praeger, New York, Westport, Connecticut, London, 1987.

Spaas, Lieve (ed.), *Echoes of Narcissus*, Berghahn Books, New York, Oxford, 2000.

Tripp, Charles and Roger Owen (eds.), *Egypt under Mubarak*, Routledge, London and New York, 1989.

Van Dam, Nikolaos, *The Struggle for Power in Syria: Politics and Society under Asad and the Ba'th Party*, I. B. Tauris, London, 2011.

Weber, Max, 'Politics as Vocation,' Speech delivered in Germany, January 1919, http://www.ne.jp/asahi/moriyuki/abukuma/weber/lecture/politics_vocation.html

Weiss, Walter M., Hg. *Die Arabischen Staaten: Geschichte – Politik – Religion – Gesellschaft – Wirtschaft* (Ed. *The Arab States: History – Politics – Religion – Society – Economy*), Palmyra, Heidelberg, 2007.

Wirth, Hans-Jürgen, *Narcissism and Power: Psychoanalysis of Mental Disorders in Politics*, translation by Ingrid Lansford (*Narzißmus und Macht, Zur Psychoanalyse seelischer Störungen in der Politik*), Psychosozial-Verlag, Giessen, 2002, 2009.

Wöhler-Khalfallah, *Der islamische Fundamentalismus, der Islam und die Demokratie: Algerien und Tunesien: Das Scheitern postkolonialer 'Entwicklungsmodelle' und das Streben nach einem ethischen Leitfaden für Politik und Gesellschaft* (*Islamic Fundamentalism, Islam and Democracy: Algeria and Tunisia: The Failure of Post-colonial 'Development Models' and the Striving for an Ethical Guide to Politics and Society*), VS Verlag für Sozialwissenschaften, Wiesbaden, 2004.

Zahler, Kathy A., *The Assads' Syria*, Twenty-First Century Books, Minneapolis, 2010.

Ziadeh, Radwan, *Power and Policy in Syria: The Intelligence Services, Foreign Relations and Democracy in the Modern Middle East*, I. B. Tauris, London, 2011.

Index